Flashlight

Flashlight

New and Selected Poems by Gayl Teller

Cherry Grove Collections

Published by Cherry Grove Collections
P.O. Box 541106
Cincinnati, OH 45254-1106

ISBN: 978-1-62549-331-6

Poetry Editor: Kevin Walzer
Business Editor: Lori Jareo

Visit us on the web at www.cherry-grove.com

Acknowledgments

The author wishes to thank the editors of the following publications in which many of these poems originally appeared, some in different versions:

New Poems
Prosopisia: An International Journal of Poetry and Creative Writing, Long Island Quarterly: 25th Anniversary Edition, RCC MUSE, October Hill Magazine, Nassau County Poet Laureate Society Review, Bards Annual, Front Range Review, The Seventh Quarry: Swansea Poetry Magazine, Long Island Quarterly, Odyssey, Performance Poets Literary Review, Bards Against Hunger: 5th Anniversary Issue, October Hill Magazine, Qutub Minar Magazine: An International Literary Magazine, Leaves of me... (Early Lilacs Press) and *Poets to Come: A Poetry Anthology in Celebration of Walt Whitman's Bicentennial* (Local Gems Press).

At the Intersection of Everything You Have Ever Loved
San Diego Poets Press, 1989
Caesura, Compassion Magazine, The Connecticut Writer, Dog River Review, Lyrical Fiesta, New Voices, Northland Quarterly, Phoebus, Pikestaff Forum, The Reading Series: K-Bar Press, A Shout in the Street, South Coast Poetry Journal, Suburban Wilderness Press, Swamp Debs, Wide Open, Wyoming: The Hub of the Wheel, NFSPS Award, Peninsula Library Award, Artemis Award, World of Poetry Award, Catalogued in Bern Porter Collection of Contemporary Letters: Miller Library, Colby College, ME

Shorehaven
Mellen Poetry Press, 1996
*Atom Mind, Dominion Review, Half Tones to Jubilee, Hudson Valley
Echoes, Long Island Quarterly, Moving Out, Phoebe, Poetry in
Performance: City College of NY, Spring: The Journal of the E.E.
Cummings Society, Bronx Visions: Bx County Historical Society,
Bronx Accent: Rutgers University Press, National League of American
PEN Women Award,* Edgar Allan Poe Prize for Literary Excellence

One Small Kindness
Plain View Press: Austin, TX, 2003
*Crone's Nest, Ezine, Performance Poets Literary Review, Long Island
Quarterly, The Mac Guffin, Reiki Manual, The Sow's Ear Poetry
Review, Spring: The Journal of the E.E. Cummings Society, Moving
Day: Premier Poets Chapbook Series, Newsday*

Inside the Embrace
Cherry Grove/ WordTech, 2010
*For Loving Precious Beast: Purple Sage Press, Harmony: 5th World
Congress of Poets for Poetry Research and Recitation—Silla Gold
Crown World Peace Literature Prize, Seoul, Korea, Long Island
Sounds, Paumanok: Poetry and Pictures of Long Island: Cross-
Cultural Communications, Songs of Seasoned Women: Quadrasoul, A
Taste of Poetry: Walt Whitman Birthplace Association, Toward
Forgiveness: Writer's Ink—NY State Council on the Arts
Decentralization Arts Grant, NY Poetry Forum Spiritual Awakening
Prize*

Hidden in Plainview
Cherry Grove/ WordTech, 2015
Bards Annual, Central Conference of American Rabbis Journal: Reform Jewish Quarterly— Gender and Judaism in Conversation, Freshet, Literary House Review/ A Hudson View Poetry Digest, Nassau County Poet Laureate Society Review, Paterson Literary Review, Performance Poets Association Literary Review, Poem, Poetrybay: Long Island Quarterly, Poet's Art, Praxis: Journal of Gender and Cultural Critiques, Sow's Ear Poetry Review, Seventh Quarry: Swansea Poetry Magazine, Long Islander: Walt's Corner, Long Island Sounds, Paumanok Interwoven: Island Sound Press, The Second Genesis: An Anthology of Contemporary World Poetry— Ajmer, India, Whispers and Shouts: Local Gems, Westmoreland Arts & Heritage Prize, Poets in Nassau Storycorps, Bellmore Library, Selection, League of Professional Theatre Women 30th Year Celebration Feature— Cherry Lane Theatre, NYC

The author wishes to thank the staff of the Plainview, NY, Mid-Island Y JCC, especially Beverly Gilbert, Cultural Arts Director, and all the wonderful poets for their dedicated support for the Poetry Reading Series, which she has had the privileged honor to direct for the past twenty-three years. The series has been found to be among the top fifty longest-running poetry series in America.

Cover photograph: "Caitlyn's Eye"
        Freeport Arts Council Photography Award
        Robert Harrison

For Mike, Paul, Maxine, Aviva, Joshua

Books by Gayl Teller

At the Intersection of Everything You Have Ever Loved

Shorehaven

One Small Kindness

Inside the Embrace

Hidden in Plainview

Edited by Gayl Teller

Toward Forgiveness: An Anthology of Poems (New York State Council on the Arts 2010 Decentralization Grant for the Arts)

Table of Contents

From *Inside the Embrace*

FLASHLIGHT

to reach out like a flashlight to illuminate wider and wider swaths of reality and the essential truths of the human condition
> From "Poet Profile: Gayl Teller"
> *The Seventh Quarry: Swansea Poetry Magazine*
> (Summer/ Autumn, 2017)

NEW POEMS

Through My Telescope

Through the telescope in my mind,
        I believe,
lighting past the horizon in the dark,
out there, in unimaginable vastness,
        the cosmos—
with all those exoplanets, the weirdly hot,
so hot, they could melt glass, and rain glass,
so cold, all earthly organisms would freeze,
those in wonky orbits at weird angles to each other,
even many and varied sibling earths.
Through the telescope in my mind,
        I am
a time traveler, through the lens on humanity,
I see history often told as the story of wars,
the gathered refuse
of wondrously limited beings,
so capable of constructing prophetic scopes,
deciphering ahead, and back to Big Bang beginnings,
all too often trapped inside dark desires,
inside that same Neanderthal cave.
As I aim my instrument for entering that
        vast imagined space—
perhaps in a galaxy far, far away,
yet strangely familiar, as looking out
        is looking in,
perhaps around some calmer, red dwarf star,
where there has been enough time, more time than we've
ever known on our young, little blue marble in space,
somewhere over that evolving rainbow, even more than
extraterrestrial intelligence, it's extraterrestrial empathy,
        I believe.

The Intelligence Bridge

"We call that the Intelligence Bridge,"
our tour guide Petr stops to point,
as he steers us through Prague.
"Such a city of castles and concerts!" I say
and get reprimanded for using "Czechoslovakia."
"It's the Czech Republic now, since '93!" he
turns, smiles generously at my inattentiveness.
"It was built by doctors, writers, teachers,
by the educated arrested for thought crimes,
like wanting to leave the country,
by those who refused to lead a double-think life—
toeing the Communist line in public,
thinking on their own in private,
by those who dared take liberties with restrictions,
who wrote and spoke the bitterness in their mouths,
but as they built, they couldn't escape
their unstoppable dream—freedom. …
Then they forced them to work in uranium mines!
Notice," he points, "only one set of tracks—
a train can go only one way at once.
You're either free or you're not!"

What does it mean to be free?
I muse on genes you're born with,
family, culture you're born into,
all the givens of experience you never chose,
givens that can click genes on and off,
and in our republic, all those terrified children
wrenched away from their parents, no records,
their deplorable train going only one way.

"What does it mean to be free?" I ask aloud.
Petr takes out his smart phone,
shows me his freedom at his fingertips—
"There," he smiles, "can you see,
on that motorcycle in Austria's grand alps,
where it's so big, there, look how wide,
that dot, there, that's me, can you see?"

Petr's father remembered the Prague Spring,
a river of liberalization rising 7 months in '68,
squelched beneath the heavy Warsaw troops and tanks,
the land gone sodden with meaningless deaths…

Cruelty is such a bewildering wilderness,
where roaming can never be completely free,
for cruelty knows only loss.
I think of those bridge builders, holding on,
unsupported at the extremities, buffeted by winds
to shape a span that would outlast them,
overlooking that swirling gap in human empathy,
but only the dead are completely not free,
for they cannot change,
while imprisonment perceives possibilities,
and cruel taskmasters teach unknowingly
the worth of kindness that spans the whole human country.

To My Friend Eileen

I'm sorry Eileen,
wherever you are, here
you were, always it seemed
in my after-school playroom,
my next-door girlfriend,
heads taller, feet wider, years younger,
snagged, gagged, giggling
in our many melodramatic thickets,
me mostly spellcaster,
you mostly spellbound.

I'm sorry Eileen,
wherever you are, here
you are again, doorbell,
"Oh, it's only you."
"That's no way to greet someone,"
my dad admonished,
and I set the terms, two sheets,
a thin pencil for you,
the fat black crayon for me,
the first to fill a page would win,
"on your mark," I was set
to congratulate myself,
but facts refract time's different hues,
like seeing sunset reds later.

I'm sorry Eileen,
wherever you are, hear
your mother Tillie yelling,
"Look what you did to her!"
your nose bleeding onto my page

for filching my formidable crayon,
your uncrying silence dripping red
tracks through our hallway,
history unrecorded to your door.

Wherever you are, "Oh,
it's only you," hear Tillie
yelling at our elation's oversudsing
whole families of cloth dolls
in the sink, spritzing ourselves silly,
hear ourselves yelling up
to your courtyard window,
"Tillie, throw down a ball, a fan,
ice-cream money, tissues for Eileen's nose."

"Oh, it's only you."
I'm sorry Eileen, hear
Tillie yelling, "Wherever is she?
Why did you leave her waiting
to walk home with you from school?"
"When is Eileen coming home?"
I missed you every summer in the country,
bored on the stoop, I waited…,
"Oh, it's only you" after you returned.

I'm sorry Eileen,
wherever you are, here I am
witness to my own misgivings, ungivings,
but also to our blazing joys,
our sordid scrapes with knees, parents, witches,
in our thickets, long overgrown,
our ice-cream cone passing like a kiss.

Remodeling

It is rising upon the rooftop
       Now become the new floor
A more private room to think in
       To rearrange the same old stuff
On more capacious shelving
       More space to hang up one's triumphs
And put in their places dreaded defeats
       All worked on reinforced skeletal walls
Windows' whole new vista to see through
       To look out upon the street of neighbors
Reframing their own horizons
       Building new baby rooms
Walking is remodeling
       Rethinking the central colors
The clashes and what will cohere
       So everywhere lived looks brand new

Doing a Jigsaw Puzzle Together

What is this appeal of irregular pieces?—
an eye of the loon? or a luminous leaf
on a branch backlit by cabin light?
or does it fit into the lake's freestyle strokes
as water sees into the sky's other side?
We walk around our table again,
reappraising what's in hand,
trying out each other's angles.
Poised on alertness's edge, at no time at all,
we sort out the frame first, wonder,
how did all these hours pass?
as double straight-backs shape corners
to hold these many variables as one whole,
together, oh the gratifying pleasure
of working out a preformed picture,
the sliding into a shared tradition's
well-wrought ease, as our bodies' gliding
into each other's comfy, cozy crevices,
on the supportive frame of our bed.

Dishwasher Duet

Loading a dishwasher is no simple task
when he helter-skelters plates,

unscraped of raveling, pasty tapestries
of pastry crumbs and salmon flakes,

and later, I swipe, wipe, reposition each
to face north, as if by some magneto-vision—

"You need more room for spoons!" he advises,
and overtakes two northerly plates

to face and scrape against each china's grain,
squeezes in a sticky bowl on a diagonal,

lays a small saucer flat on its back,
and later, opening, I laugh at our clash,

but move back the plates up against the rack,
restation all short-stemmed glasses

onto the shallower upper shelf—
So it goes, the way we each load a domestic rack

alludes to the way we each have been loaded,
slanted by ancient codes long ago, and ever since,

something like a long marital conversation,
often seeming to lack any pattern,

but inside, the braided currents share
a cascading, humming lore of love,

and as the heated waters settle down,
the beautiful underhues do come clear.

Along Highway One

(for Mike)

Celebrating fifty years of marriage
is like standing in a poem
in the stillness of the snowy egret,
poised on its own reflection,
in the pool of mirrors we saw
as we journeyed on the switchback trail
from LA to Monterey,
then on to the San Francisco Bay.
Others have tripped closer to the edge—
We took the inside track, the surer grip.
Our legs wrapped around each other,
a knowing familiarity, naked security.
Each day in walking away
to our various businesses,
we've carried each other's fingerprints,
all over our bodies, a visceral blanket by now
given in the spirit of triage
like mental health workers.
You need it rounding these white-knuckle
bends on life's scary mountainsides, climbing years
higher into the northern sky,
the horizon growing wider, vaster,
farther away, until this view—
our life on a postcard,
or looking out from a window in a plane.

Landscape at such height knits,
like fifty years together out on an overlook—
with even the waves crashing against
our ancient massive idiosyncrasies
jutting out like glacial boulders when we were young—

Now one panorama. Such loveliness in serenity.
So much safer because we share the driving
along the hairpin turns, the curve-hugging,
jaw-dropping miles, with each of our years
seeking to be made welcome in some all-inclusive,
ecumenical congregation called marriage,
some say an endangered species,
while all too often our years have been
more like these many massive elephant seals
tossing sand on their torsos,
splayed out and heaving on time's vast beach,
barking and sparring for place:
How to make welcome and include
the time I came home from the hospital
with our baby with the time you came home
from the hospital with a catheter with the time
we left together for the marriage counselor with
the times we left our parents in the hospitals.
And then everywhichway we turn our heads,
something so beautiful, so unphotogenic
as these playful otters as entangled in kelp
as our lifetime friends entangled in our years,
as this giant artichoke flower rising
purple as our passion in a secret garden
where we giggle and renew our vows,
and already I am longing for you—
fifty years are not enough.

A Forest Walk

In our worn shoes, each step
is a muckraker, as we go
slogging and slushing through
the organic ooze of this vast forest,
her house on its cusp,
my niece Jen, a new mom,
with her mom Joyce, who is
my sister and grandmother to Alexa,
and me, great-aunt, sister, and aunt,
in this totem slurping through old
leaf bits, pulverized with rust,
mites, and petals' color-specks,
dropped buds, unopened
as our own shut-off genes,
we'll never know about,
an unfathomable crush
of unrealized disease and dreams,
each step sinking us deeper
into pleasure splattered with repulsion,
as we "Cooo!" at Alexa, "Ooo!" at the muck,
pull at our coats, laugh with each other.
Even without her arthritis, my sister's
plodding is like pushing a carriage
through mud after menopause.
In our sister-bonding car ride,
from New York to Philly, radio on,
we could barely abide that sinking feeling
in the organic ooze of human news,
more bombs and beheadings,
alongside early childhood program plans.

Jen says, "There's great-aunt, grandmother,
great-grandmother, so why is there
no word for great mother?"
"That's because motherhood
means on-the-job training!" we reassure,
when she confesses she's depressed.
"Could be hormone withdrawal,
sleep deprivation, who knows!"
"Or the sadness gene of our cousins,"
whispers my sister, one having begged her
to come hide all her knives
when her first baby was born.
And high on a cushion like a queen
in her carriage, Alexa gurgles and giggles,
her mouth agape with words
that just won't take shape,
her wide open, blue-grey eyes
soaking up the sky of snow and spring,
as we, like worker bees,
primp and tickle her attention
to be and go her worthwhile way
through all the labor love pushes and plods her to.

Once Upon a Virtual Afternoon

Around the kitchen's granite-topped island,
family central, each sits, unspeaking,
each looking down in reverence
at an electronic device, 4 of them laid out,
their bold letters dark and compelling
like granite headstone etchings.

She's young and in love with a lush, liquid stain
lipstick she untests on a finger, orders with a click,
hangs out with her best friend on her smartphone,
Snapchats a shot of her goofy brother
fingering his shaky tooth back and forth,
and her friend snaps back one of her dad, mouth open.
As best friends, they snap each other every day
to get their Snapchat rewards with dopamine surges.
Then she texts her how she danced for an hour
with "the cutest partner ever" on X Box.

Her brother is zapping dragons and monsters,
scoring higher and higher, as more and more
reincarnate in some compulsion loop app.

His mom deletes the split-screen faces
on a conference call completed, unusual for a Sunday,
on "Strategies Enhancing Sensitivity in Public Schools."
She untouches the lace on the blouse,
unfeels the fluff of the cashmere,
unscents the orange blossom fragrance,
unanswers the landline's ringing,
lets voicemail tell whomsoever—

"We seldom answer this phone.
Please hang up and text us." And so
her father, states away, sends his message
one more state removed, "like Plato's shadows
to the real, like *Reader's Digest* version
of *Gone With the Wind,*" he teaches,
"like freeze-dried astronaut food
to mom's delicious stroganoff! And we can't
get Skype to hold Little Guy's whole face!"—

As she unhears his voice as he types, she continues
to roam the airless, high-end e-boutiques
of luxury e-tailers along the virtual boulevard,
then checks again for a burst of warmth
and affirmation from a Facebook like.

Her husband reads a news feed
like an exitless maze, structured
so one page path leads down to another
and another and another, till he yawns
silently, opens his online course, reads
the unheard remarks of an unmet professor,
how he should "learn how a sentence works."

Each one on the island unhears as a computer
tells voicemail, "Our records indicate
you have not updated your free Google account."
From inside, the little one rouses, cries to be held.

Posted on Facebook/ Poem

Husband—My challenge to my family:
        Let's go 24 hours WITHOUT
        ordering anything from amazon.com.
        I know it'll be an epic struggle,
        but let's give it a try!
        What say you, wife?

Wife—Yeah! I just can't commit to that.
        If our household didn't need any items,
        then I would not order anything…
        mind you, these are not frivolous purchases,
        but more like light bulbs, Ziplock bags,
        and parts of Halloween costumes.

Husband's Mother/Poet Aloud to Her Husband—
        I just don't get it: Why do they
        make their private topic public?

Mother/Poet's Conscience In Private—
        Why is your son's private topic
        made open to the public on Facebook
        any different from your making
        it public in your own poem?

Poet On String Theory

The baker places my macaroon cake
inside a cardboard box,
then places the box in a device
where he pushes a button,
and inside a second or two,
it's all tied up with string,
all the flaps tucked in
securely, no loose ends.

I'd like to put a poem in there,
so I could see it all hold together,
no mixed-metaphor flaps sticking out,
and I could finally stop retyping
because I'd know the poem is complete.

Better yet, I'd like to put my whole
precancer condition inside there,
feel the benumbed finishing string
wrap securely all around me,
so I could be sure the GYN got it
all, and all of me is holding together.

Hussein

It's the outset of a new spring semester—
he leaves his class, flags me down!
I remember his name, my former student,
who'd made our tears flow in the dead of winter
with his family memoir— abandoned by his mother,
losing his grandmother who raised him,
his struggles to feel his mother's struggles
the icebreaker, as he cleared emotional space
to review her fate anew, and forgave her
for all of us encircling with him
in a writing skills course, how he'd
generously speak during a discussion lull,
good naturedly reposition chairs for the next group.
So glad to see him, I reach for his arms,
then resist the untraditional hug,
but feel it in his friendly eyes.
What are we going to do!?
I know he means the travel ban
on seven majority Muslim countries.
I'm just an Allport "label of primary potency"!
I'm thinking of changing my name!
he almost laughs. *It's a shrieking siren!*
One of my friends was arrested right from his home!
If I leave the country to see my brother,
will I be banned from re-entry?
I tell him about our advocacy programs,
the new Deportation Defense Clinic,
the petitions I'd signed to Ban the Ban,
with the old Trail of Tears, McCarthy years,
internment camps escaping into the new term's air.

I've wondered what it means to know my country
by my hand on the chalk to a blackboard,
at the heart of a classroom,
like a silent pledge of allegiance
to young, impressionable eyes
that have seen Gene Forrester's *blind ignorance*
when he made his best friend fall from a tree.
Is a country that one human heart writ large,
or the many making a synergistic light?
And *what's in a name*? It's the one word
that refers to the whole person.
To this kind kindred spirit, I'd choose to be
my brother, my parting words, I know too lame,
Don't change your name, Hussein! Don't change your name.

Guilt

I'd like to stay outside awhile and just
watch the petunias plunging in peace…
I ask myself, Is that all right?
Can I just let the red dazzling dahlias'
giant heads overwhelm my thoughts?
I love the feel of these last azaleas
filling me into their fuchsia felicities…
So why isn't my empathy enough?
While colleagues gather at Lincoln Center
to march for faithful charge of this earth,
while women rally to maintain their domain
over their own eminent wombs,
I'd like to stay outside awhile and be
beyond the claspers, harassers, safe at home.

Rock Sonnet

What is this beauty of boulder enveloping
my view, as if a fisherman within his line
untouched? Potential floods me with energy!
The craggy, massive stillness has me—I'm hooked.
Irregular in shape, dull dun in hue,
it doesn't belong in a poem meant for love,
yet craggy, retired teachers, out in the sun,
know, with no lesson to make, no agenda,
abraded by long transport and weathered in place,
how silent majesty sits, center of attention,
where a yellow finch feeds on fluff seeds
dropped by a skinny tree grasping for life.
and two orange-blossomed lovers kiss,
all brethren born in supernova breath.

The Girl Who Confided in a Goldfish

She wrote in her college journal as a kid
how she'd rush home from the school bus stop,
push open the door to see her best friend
Corolina, her orange fish with white little patches
swimming in the diamond tank with golden stones,
sometimes hiding inside the small yellow castle aglow,
how she'd feed her and tell her all she'd done that day,
hidden behind the bold outcries kids made at play,
bearing their bold tongues as they spoke up with answers,
answers she really knew but for the words,
how she'd thought this was going to be her life,
happily swimming her news out into Corolina's tank
whenever she came home, the kids gone long and far
across the bold sea to neighborhood parks and sunfields—
till Corolina went bobbing, belly-up …
and the yellow castle got stashed away
with her secrets boxed and shelved in the dark hall closet.

The girl who confided in a goldfish, a college freshman
who had traveled farther than she remembered
to live in a dorm, under the tread of strangers,
where she was keeping an empty fish tank with a yellow castle,
where summoning shadows went swimming in and out,
as she wrote in her college journal as a kid
how she could still feel the backs of their legs
pressing up against her as freely they talked
about their pets, that gushing over a French poodle,
how intolerable the goldfish crackers stuffed in their mouths
and the boy who'd also lost his fish who said,
"Man, why can't my parents get me a lion or dragon!"

I can still see her there, so early, waiting,
the girl who confided in a goldfish still swimming
inside the college freshman, wrapped in her winter coat,
so long before the other students arrived, waiting
for me to unlock the small castle of a classroom aglow,
such a big responsibility, more than I knew,
how I'd become Corolina, her goldfish.

Alexa

Because she turned the superhero upside down
and placed the small soccer ball in my hand,
because she held his feet to her shoulder
and pointed purposefully at the ball, so I knew,
and I threw the ball at the superhero's legs—
Because she whacked it! Made it fly—
like a winged seed splitting open with my joy—
more than I thought a 3 year old could,
because she stood there in inches of kiddie pool water
in just a diaper and sun, unharnessed
of how the vintage game has to be played,
and made contact again! And again!
Because she put the superhero upside down in my hand,
pitched the little soccer ball to me,
and jump-cheered Hoorayeee! when I hit it!
Because she turned loose in a wide open space
of her own making, running in her own
hazardous heaven, too young to even think
about what she would someday miss…
Because she made me see there's so much life—
Her giggle! Her bow! Her wacky sense of in-place-ness!

At the Ceremony

We sat overlooking the sun-sprayed spouts,
all rising, higher, rainbowed, ethereal,
over the jagged coastline boulders
and rocks stacked, just so, by human hands,
and left in the wake of their esthetic feel,
all rising, family, friends, in sparkly garb,
in gaiety sparked at the solemn auspiciousness,
all rising, embedded in the wafts of moistened grass,
turning to them, two young men, on their standing ground,
healing together as they walked on ancient woven roots,
up the path of earthly promise for life, renewal,
such a natural validation to make each more real,
to create a home within each other, all of us
were elevated, as they were pronounced "married."

Thoughts at My Granddaughter's Bat Mitzvah

Let us pray to the high moral ground
that we each think we hold,
that none of us holds,
that we can hardly see.
Let our arms open fire
around each other
with human healing.
Let us not turn to stone at the carnage,
O the carnage of lost focus
trailing from trucks trampling babies,
terror-by-explosive ignorance,
pressure-cooker poverty,
Jim Crow arms that tear flesh two ways,
chronic unemployment, abysmal educational opportunities,
social dislocation, prejudice, indifference.
Let us pray in the religion where we breathe
deeper through the other,
as if in a vacationaire,
walking along a marginal way
along each other's coastline of splendors.
Let us see the grandeur of an ocean
teeming with life inside
each outcast.
If we take care of our own,
let us remember our blood ties.
Let us see the abducted girl in Nigeria
as the girl kidnapped from our family ward.
We are each other's own.
Let us pray to what shamanism, Judaism, Hinduism,
Buddhism, Taoism, Islam,
Confucianism, Christianity, and atheism have in common—

a need to be consoled, protected,
an escape from absurdity, despair,
communion.
Let us revere life as sacred connection.
Let us share without dividing the enjoyment
of each enhanced by the enjoyment of all.
Let us pray to our likeness
shedding light on our grand mystery.
Let us remember Luca,
of 4 billion years ago,
our venerable common ancestor of all living things.
In the logic of my prayer
perhaps this can save us,
that somehow we see we are still that
single cell
precariously clinging to a volcanic sea vent.

(Luca, the Last Universal Common Ancestor, a cell of 4 billion years ago, believed to be the ancestor of all life, emerged in a sea vent)

From *At the Intersection of Everything You Have
Ever Loved*

Lace

Where the overarching oak was frail
  lace shadow in intimacy
    with our own, we sat,
      my mother and I,

idly watching the wind break patterns
  that would not sit still
    with us, any more than
      we could sit there

in the house full of well-wishing
  strangers after the funeral.
    If not for the gaps,
      the lace before us

would have had no loveliness.
  On the ground we tended,
    the negative spaces
      held sunlight

the way you can love a person right through
  the shortcomings. She fed me
    wild berries plucked
      from the shadows,

and like the child that I wasn't, I trusted
  she knew which were poisonous.
    We partook of the sweetblack
      fruit of the tanglevine

together, and on impulse, I thanked her
   for my love of nature. She had died
      so many times in her life,
         her heart understood

the pre-fall tremblings of the tiger lily
   anthers at their peak of pollen.
      With a straight-pin, she kept
         the black lace to her head.

Handfast

Like the leaf that has lost the forest
at the end of the endless summer,

I am a long way from home, a long way
from that radiance that burned

a circular band of pallor beneath my wedding ring,
long worn, on the weakest finger of my weaker hand.

This is the blanched track of love
expecting too much of itself,

casting a shadow over my entire body.
Did I wear its star-rapt filigree down

with too constant wearing? I never
could take it off, not for 17 years,

not when I was alone with your letters,
constant as pulsars from basic training's separation,

not when I bathed our baby's raw umbilicus and convulsive fevers,
not when I cleared the table, scraping

the meat-encrusted forks from our mouths,
not when there was such heavy silence in the limbs

of our lovemaking, nor knuckle deep in the manure
in our garden growing salad greens and love-lies-bleeding

in amaranthine memory with drooping spikes,
our curses and caresses grown indistinguishable

in the mulch of our years together,
not even when it was the only thing left

till my nakedness and I loved another man.
At the end of basic training, as new wife,

when you came home passionate and pale—
so much thinner than the husband I had conjured,

I learned the other kind of separation in your returning crush,
the worst loneliness in reunion was separation from a dream.

But now I take off this ring,
now that each bombarding micron of our lives

has worn down its decorative Florentine
to this shiny, thin smoothness of itself,

now that each bombarding micron of our lives
has burnished it like an artifact of our ancient hearts,

now that the most durable part remains.
I shiver to be so undressed and disconnected.

What is this pallid border of my life on my hand
that is so smooth, that if I keep my eyes closed,

its presence is as impalpable as the underside of a mindless
wheel that would keep me on its circular course,

making no allowances for traveling conditions,
yet having no hub of its own without my finger?

Do I keep a ghost on my hand,
The ghost of anything that claims to be solidly precious,

or as irrevocable as the heart's commitments once made?
Is this the negative space of memory's resplendent photograph,

or the pale afterimage of a moment's throbbing insight?
Yes, my heart is not a constant meter,

it skips beats, and races away, and slows down to itself,
and is haunted by that guilt.

But now I am only sorry you still believe
in that temple of separation that makes ideal lovers,

but not sinewy mates. And just when I'm sure
everything you would say to me has already been

said or lost, you ask me to tell you definitely
I no longer love you, so we might love again.

Maybe when winter blusters near I will forget
passion's radiance revealed this ghost on my hand,

but will remember the metal tie we ringed
around our avocado tree to support it in its thinness

and how that unnatural metal ring
enabled the tree to outgrow its limited hold

and became so enmeshed in its most vital tissue
that we couldn't remove that ring

without ripping apart some very essence of that tree.

Treading Water Together

He curves his lean stroking
        way toward me, puffs a cloud
breath, a visible warmth

made clearer by cold. His fears
        are warm because he says them
to me, inside shapes of fog.

It's surprisingly easy to speak
        in private water like this, no
crowd of other demands, for once.

Why don't we do this more often?
        Remember this spot. We'll pretend
we've made our mark crossing mud-

bottomed, slippery shallows,
        the jagged way of rocks and
chipping out secrets between

which twist, which ruin, pretend
        we could foresee looking back
down this channel's palpitations,

find this emotion's greening imbroglio
        in the swift currents sweeping us
along, pretend we leave tracks

in water, but who could
        inhabit the quicksand of memory
foretold? Not even now while

his familiar invisible call
        strays out more whole in hazy words
wafting softness onto his crisp

open-and-shut eye just floating on
        deep green, not even as a spectrum flits
between us, iridescently, then

invisibly in our plunging gasp.
        We kiss. What's vulnerability got
to do with love? Underbreath, under-

water, I look up at his look rippling
        in clouds. I've been afraid a long time
I'd drown to know him so.

Splash!

The Sunflower

I think it was when I found the decapitated stalk
  that I remembered how I learned to grow
my flowers indoors, on the body of my dead parakeet,
  in an 8-inch cheesebox with 3 inches of soil
scooped from the weedy fringe of a community lot,
  where boisterous little leaguers struck
    out for the beauty and terror anew.

Nothing but a bizarre weed would grow in that box
  and prolific mites casting webs of dark
tensions beneath the leaves, cut-off from circulation
  of earth minerals. I remembered, from the east
sill to the west sill, as I kept moving my weed, still,
  how hard it was to hold the light indoors—
yet that weed unabashedly bloomed one morning, a minute
  lavender I thought slipped from the breast
    of my parakeet thaumaturge, Pretty Boy.

When my father visited one afternoon last summer,
  we sat on sunchairs in the garden
beneath that big, petalled sun's-eye view,
  Pauls's only surviving sunflower,
that he'd hoed and weeded up to his window height,
  bringing a yellower light into his room.
Funny how at its height it seemed most burdened
  with the weight of its own beauty
and hunched itself inward like an old pundit
  on a sturdy stalk of vast heart-
    shaped leaves for shade.

We waved to my neighbors in their garden over a root-
  hung fence, where roses and their teenage boy
were doing their earthwork and rising in bright sun,
  outgrowing the wattled security there.
Hunched-in on his own center of secrets, my father
  asked me questions he knew the answers to,
not out of false humility, but to hide what mattered
  to him, or to preserve what had taken him
his life to know he knew. He asked me if I knew
  why that handsome boy so often wore
    a gawky cap so low on his face,

I told him what I knew about when their boy was seven,
  a little younger than Paul, with a head
of copious ringlets, golden as corn silk, how just
  about when boys grow strangely aware
of themselves, and he was prattling over some immense
  escapade of his, two men yanked him
by his hair down the backstairs behind the movies,
  shaved off his boyhood curls, and as they
made him drop his pants, they made him retch
  down his hair so he'd never forget
    the initiation into his beauty.

My father warned me how intolerable the sunlight,
  his grandson shouldn't saunter off
in it. I thought I could never ask Paul to
  ensconce his flowers in a cheesebox
with a plastic's pure soil, nor to try
  to balance a box of transient sun
    on such a narrow sill.

My father's face was more parchment than before,
  tan-wizened, bald-pated like an old
sunflower disk not yet ready to release its seeds
  that weighted it, shorter, but riper
than before. Space shrank before his eyes
  as I watched him fall into himself,
    into his own heavy memories.

Whoever it was must have come late at night,
  when boundaries get swallowed whole,
whoever it was must have brought a saw,
  or an ax, and hacked hard to spirit
off that unripened disk that wouldn't grow
  on anyone else's stalk
    but Paul's.

What Is This Pull-Over?
(From My Son)

What's wrinkled with detaching warmth—
warmth yet brooding in the tucked plush
fabric from the heart of fresh muffins,
and mittens just flipped to the floor
with a careless suspender just draggling,
chinkitty-chankitty across a kitchen
that is no longer there, with a window
to the snowman in the yard, his beet eyes
bleeding backwards through his head, the way
my blood seeps through the frozen image?

"Would you wear it, ma?" he smirked.

What's hanging loosely about my breasts
to be tucked in to some shadowy place—
place that keeps sliding on breath's
rising, falling, crescendo, decrescendo,
the edging popping out around him,
a flapping from that sense of being, a soloist,
and we rose applauding in the auditorium,
the burgundy seams still bound tight,
precluding how winter light would window
through each pore in the thready binding
of this passed-on pull-over from my son
to dazzle and chill to my bone?

A Picture Horology
   (For My Son)

Having no need
but to be torn and torn
anew from sheet after sheet of self,

from the eidetic European bridge whose arches

never complete themselves but go on forever down
in photographed stone, or in what we believe

is something strong and supportive
as stone uprights under the family on the bridge,
disappearing down in the bottomless water, the calendar

that hangs by a thread in his room, like its water,

has no picture all its own
but takes on and lets go whatever looks into it.

And that is how the gurus tell you to get out of bed
to a new morning, to tear away the sheets
to whatever picture you never quite suspected,

for we tell time by pictures.

It takes on and lets go whatever his magic
marker red-circles around its blind square eyes,

whatever raw blue skies get cut with red clay
rooftops and cobblestone roads where he's never been
that enter and admit the shape of his indelible wind

as he drums his snare, there in his music's growing

tangle of the everywhere of the not-here
and throbs with the calendar's distance in his eyes.

It was too soon to be torn
from my warm sheets,
but early that morning he untucked me

and yanked off the one with the solid red tulips

to his all new tableau vivant I couldn't believe
was he standing there in a dim glimmering light

cut with his elegance in a charcoal tuxedo, flaming
red cummerbund, sharp patent leather shoes, glossy as water
around his feet, and the piercing edge

of unexpected perception. There the familiar archway

still delicately suspended over his darkling eyes. There
the hieratic stance of lost boyhood, the classic posture

that splintered in the waters gathering
in the breathless moment
my eyes dared fully yield

at his admission.

And if I had the strength I would have run
for the camera, or for something, but

as usual, there would have been no preparation made,
no film to condense from that auroral glimmering
what was not visible, and never would be again—

but in split-seconds, as when he grabbed my hand

forgetting his guard, on the curdling brink
of his seat in a movie house,

and I felt each stripling finger gently
withdraw itself to its own
hand that had been the shadow clock of mine

to indicate it was time, was time.

Jack-O'-Lanterns at Their Doors

They flock together in an endless chain, extending themselves
all the way across Pelham Parkway on blister-wood benches,
the elderly Jews in felt hats, blotting up some sun, and lambskin
toppers, puffing out their chests with cigars and talk
of their children. Another harvest of light is almost through.
The trees have rusted around them. Like the pigeons, they
have come for the sun and the gathering of their kind
on this shortgrowing fall day, as they bicker over who
sits where in the sun. Ready to defend themselves, they come
armed with parched snapshots their clicking cameras shed
like yellow leaves, and laminations of what their children
made them, and their children's children's broken SWAK seals.

They are the family historians, the narrators of the Bx romance.
As the wax is gathered in their ears—sealing them in—
with a rush of blood come nutrients washed up from beneath
—kosher pickles swimming in the spiced barrel eyes of a child
—Moishe's pushcart—lunch apples for a nickel—riding free
and sockless—standing in the moving Westchester Avenue trolley
—hitchhiking the night away up West Farms Road—holding money
in your open hands in the open air—the Forward reading
backward on a slow-shuttered reel of an autumn afternoon.

With hands that interrupt the tremors of the linden trees,
¼ in English, ¾ in Yiddish, the story gets told on some
Parkway bench every sunny afternoon, winked at by a grandchild
every last Sunday of the month. O the way their Bronx used to be.
Their eyes move back and forth on mere sunthreads,
as if under some mobile swinging linked shapes to hold—to hold
—to stare—to grasp—to sleep—to sleep—to shuttle back
along darker tracks—rattling and banging with sense-chafing blasts
they don't tell the grandchildren about, except as gentle tales
of subterranean afternoons, riding without reason, nor need
for one, back and forth, back and forth on the 42nd St. shuttle.

Yarmulkes and kerchiefs have absorbed lost colors of their hair,
colors they find again stained in glass in the shul, burning
slowly through the leaves. The Yahrzeit candle glows, indifferent
to their debates—"My mother, may she rest in peace, has always
looked down on me,"—sighs Emma, her head shaking involuntarily.
"And is she with her mother, who is with her mother, who is with
her mother, and so on, and so on, back to Eve?"—mocks Aaron.

Lidded pillboxes dangle their time-measured wholeness
in powdered grains, deep in their pockets, where all the loves
of their lives pulverize into a moment's sudden warmth
on a bench in the sun. In this living so long on Pelham Parkway,
they have come to mimic the local trees—some have bristles
and spines, and some are S-shaped and bare. Their limbs are
freeing to themselves again, their work is done, the draining
radiance is sinking into itself. And some have come to scatter
crusts, whistling for feathers that flutter from beyond
the split branches—"Here Mercury! Here Snowflake! Ooo—
Did you think I wouldn't come for you today? Mama's here."

I find the bench where my grandmother used to display her
hundred-hour volunteer buttons and badges, gold-winged service
pins for her twenty years at the Beth Abraham Home for unwanted
incurables, spoonfeeding the armless, sponging the listless.
A man with hyaline eyes offers me a seat—"Life is like
a hydra," he philosophizes with both hands. "You cut off one
problem, a new one grows." I try to follow, through his
articulate fingers, the indelible number on his wrist, and white
bandages around his ankles, swollen and deadlocked
like all his chrysalis lives that never hatched in his spring.
His children are cruising the Mediterranean out of Piraeus—
"getting their dollar's worth in drachmas and baklava!"—

She spoke with both hands too—of red jelly-filled candies—
large bow tie cookies—hand-woven baskets for bread—raisins
spilling over from coffee tins—and even then in her flower-
print robe that loosened away from her body—she held out
the double cartons of orange juice she stashed for us
from the nursing home pilferers in case we were thirsty—

He advises me to keep some money in a Swiss bank as he
recalls 5000 marks slipped as an offering into a tailor's
slammed books—"'Nicht genug!' Think it can't happen here?"
We watch the wind herd the clouds across the Parkway sky
like some vast seasonal migration. A room with a view
of the Parkway is a blessing when that certain white light
breaks rainbow upon each wound in the glass, and the stained
window opens out upon this little grass island, surrounded
by an asphalt sea, a faint redolence of a distant skin burning.

Doing a push-up off his mahogany cane, a man stakes his place
in the migration of canes across the Parkway. Leaves crack
to mosaic bits under his feet as he goes with a friend
for a little strolling, on a wide open, grandchild-fringed
road. They welcome the level places, touch-up piecemeal
assortments from family dramas in the arcade that's never
out of season—it's a trip within a trip. …

Against the falling leaf, the wider horizon, the crisp rustle
of a newly fallen friend, a man's pace changes He can pause now
to think some thoughts unbounded by the height of the stock
market, or the brown of a woman's eyes. For time has swelled
like the gourd, detaching from the vine, carving itself
into the most grotesque jack-o'-lantern of all.

White frosted mornings vanish with grandchildren, and whispery
autumn evenings seep into their rooms. Every evening now,
the stars of eternity are more in their places, more clearly
seen, as the leaves snap from under the wax of unopened buds,
waiting on another spring. While all the eaves along the Parkway
moan a memento mori, a seat in the warm open air in this
haunted month of Halloween is a seat up front on a high holy day.

Passover Caribbe

        Thank you Emperor
for showing me my lungs
    aloud through my ears as never before, for this
      new dimension, learning by forgetting
          what I had a nose for. If I forgot
          to forget what I knew, I'd choke on my habit
of breath that had worked well
    for me for many years.
      Shiny ebony boy about 19,
          long fat braids bursting across your head,
        sweet like the black pineapple
fat ladies balanced in braided palm
    baskets still green on their heads—
      the hummingbird wings whisking
          across 15 steel drums, the trade wind
        teaching the palms to sing its song,
the hibiscus yellow breasts ringing in banana leaves,
    liting to feed from my braided breakfast mat,
        and the taste of banana-baked grouper
          all feeding into that rippling,
        where you looked up from under the glass bottom.
"I'm the Emperor," you grinned.
    I know why we sailed your name
      between the jagged reefs.
          "Whoever is chicken man have to pay twice!"
        You laughed, I would have to pay twice.
And triple for the high-collared, complaining lady.
    "This is my garden," you beamed
      and gave yourself to its swaying
          sea fan, anemone pulse,
        your flippers beating between

bright lavender lives,
      your snorkel spouting like a porpoise
          from the deep, from the whole sea's breathing
               motion. Teach me that abandon.
              Ashore, we passed the sugar mill stumps
overgrown with vines
     dipping into the salt water. Your bitter herbs,
        Your great-grandfather beaten and broken
             to make the land taste sweet.
        We drove you home
to the eaten wooden box, turquoise splashed
    on lopsided cinderblocks, a scrawny goat nursing
       by a runnel of fetid water.
              Never off the island
         and you didn't intend to leave your garden,
where you had taken the mouthpiece
    from your mouth and put it into mine,
       taught me to breathe with my ears,
           to see with ripples, how
           across your breathing batik curtain,
Emperor, we were all descendants of slaves
    on that boat, in one direction or another,
       without a ritual to learn to breathe
             deeper through the other.

Old Woman's Plot

White marble chips are her ground
she parts for peat moss, rich black humus,
the perennial remembering of a future
pinkyellow-rayed, deepset red-haloed,

day's double eye about to reopen to her
amethyst bubble of volcano. (The Greeks,
she read, believed the stone and plant
of that name could keep you sober.)

A solidified burning she juxtaposed
to the new gaillardia seeds, little
shuttlecocks from her hand to the land.
Sunflashing mica eyes she positioned

over her sinuous gully she filled with smooth
turquoise gravel, her solid Caribbean Sea,
water unmoving, better than real, attracts
no bugs to her white gypsophila, baby's breath,

breath of feathers staked and named. Still,
it's the part she can't contain she loves
the best in spite of its unruliness.
A slice of geode from Mexico, a dried overspill

of Indian paint pot, a granite piece
of Yosemite at the foot of the bridge
washed with California redwood stain.
Every stone has a thousand eyes:

this from the Bahama marketplace at the dock—
How much you want to pay for seastone, pretty lady?
with chip on bottom. *You hold upside down*;
this old brown fish rock hole

held gill breathings, now empty
gills of afternoon breathing through
her wishing well, home of a million feet
that come and go: these red-winged blackbird feet

she knows; these slimy slug trails
she can name, but others skulk beneath
her bright coral fan. Star-leaf lupines
are long pink lighthouses whose petals

point out the sun and the stars
to the stone duck on the white marble shore,
beak in arched wing, never swims away from its spot.
Correspondences of rose petals and rose quartz,

tiger lily and tiger eye, so each
staked-up bender aligns for her with its
unmovable twin. Only the wind finds
their corresponding faults. She breathes

a white lime cloud, diazinon
genocide side of beauty in her lungs,
rubs Vaseline on the rocks to preserve
the wet look of the sea in a lone

achieved stillness on her knees.
Sere of succession and sere of withering
in one word, it's all contained
without a fence, open to all to see

her succession of bloomings she's timed,
keeps beauty as long as she can.
Till frost yellow coreopses keep opening
one after another. The transparent quartz design

she can see clear through to the ground
with her one good eye. Only the shadows
sweep the sharpnesses unbruised.
Her hands are all cut up, dirt fills each wound

so ugly to make it lovely here where
there's no place to walk on this bridge,
no water to drink, no fruit to eat,
nothing useful is beautiful to her.

Northern Lights
(for Uncle Jack)

From the shoal of the ship's pool
where the dream rose as a mammoth wave,
with the sway of your excursion, the rocking
water was a warning, *Get out of the pool, Jack!*

From the floodlit hand massaging your heart
where the needle spurted adrenal fire,
with the jolt of the paddles, the lightning
startled your wind's hues, your seasoul sound awakening anew,

From the portal the purple Indian corn crossed
where you bestowed your strings and reeded winds,
with balalaika biased on your paunch, the Thanksgiving
we didn't know the song our dissonance met in music,

From the salt stick, *You should have plain, Jack!*
where your spittle huffed, *So I'll lick it off!*
with a rap to Aunt Leona's roast rump, the riding,
How can they stop me! Tell me I won't grow old?

From the obese quadruple-egg, raw onion hero
where the rotunda of your mouth opened on your dream,
with that day sanctified by the cycle, the counting,
Only 4 eggs a month, Jack!—that being the time of the month,

From the fjord's fluid shave to the glacier
where your vessel's horn shrilled off hunks of ice,
with the bloodwave's lashback as you sprawled, salted, wetfaced,
the will shimmering aurora giving unreliable illumination,

From your underground electric passage to see *Da*—cause they said
        You're Hughes' spitting image—
where you fell wheezing through a breathing hole,
with Aunt Leona's forced air your prompter, *They're coming, Jack,*
they're coming! The showgoers knelt in neon auroras. *The holding*
heart can't sleep, you muttered, and rode with the sirens again,

From your cloudwhite hospital gown, you creased a smirk
where adventure rose in Alaskan caves lined in bluish icebreaths,
with a couple you met no one else spoke to, the tundra blossoming
UJ, what spirit in you! You feigned a 5th was beneath your gown,

From the snowpeaked Parkinson tremors, the cleansing hug
where your arms' holding inlet overflooded into waves, *Goodby!*
with our kiss we were leaving again. UJ, was that the last? *The*
        vanishing
Eskimo's name-soul lives forever, you said. *He marks his grave*
        with jawbone,

From the bed where they pronounced you dead, thrice, to the bed
        you still sell
where you rose with posturepedic mattresses at Mays Department
        Store,
with 80 years *I still chase women, but I've forgotten why!* The
        jawboning
An eclipse of the sun comes once in a while, but an Eclipse mattress
        is forever,

From your see-through face sliding in-and-out the revolving
        hospital door to the golf course
where the instructors said, *You shouldn't play, Jack!* And you
        banged their backs
with bare skin. *It's almost always not now. Ghosts go where they
        will!* The teeing off
got easier past the first freeze over day-broken landscape,

From the ivory crusts on your chin, the keysong you lured, the
        walrus tusks you gloated got your signature,

From you who assumed man does not live to eat alone, so we all
        had to overeat with you,

From you who declared, *Most people's hair gets lighter with age.
        My head gets lighter!*

From you who announced, *If we eat early, I'll eat later, and if
        we eat later, I'll still eat later, and I'll die at 109
        instead of 110,*

From you who couldn't recall why you did what you did yesterday,
        but the melodies from 14,000 days lyrics ago kept making
        their promises across your keyboard,

From you who watched exuberant Eskimos dancing in Kotzebue
        on Independence Day, who held the beating membrane of
        a walrus-liver drum, who digested muktuk and absorbed
        nitroglycerin,

From you, Uncle Jack, you freelance tundra blossom, a wild
    octogenary forget-me-not, who's known the sea's
    northedge, the indomitable floe-break, the pristine lure
    of bald ice—did you hear the bells swell in light, did
    the current lead you slowly blue, did your haggard
    body haul you back as a supply-laden husky strains
    over jumbled sea ice?—

And you answer in bowstring and a vibrating wrist.

Freshman Composition
(For EG11 W1449, Temp II, Western Campus)

>There are bulldozers
over our words when we meet, and in their blatant
>>and their silent din
inside our chilly trailer, where there's no restroom
>>and no fountain
to wet our throats, as Temp IV gets razed,
>>we speak at an early hour
with the wash of sleep's soundless sea about.
>>Out on our words, we raft
toward each other's nameless strangers
>>evoked in the clouds
around the chalk's clear lines. Erasure
>>of the warm-up exercise
for consistency of person spins off a vague nebula.
>>Eloise reads aloud
her persuasive essay appealing to the authority
>>of hungry children
whose needs "got tabled unfed with the free
>>school lunch cancellation."
And Tim, wide awake as a student critic, quotes verbatim
>>the text's limitation
of such expertise based on personal testimony.
>>He talks at blackboard ghosts
of unabsorbed white words. Then once more
>>we look for the significance
of structure inside a temporary structure, and we
>>study form and function,
how Talese's "irresistible seductress" is his sibilant
>>sound. And Helga snickers,

"Growing minds should have equal rights
          to their physicality
as our words do!" and puts on her coat to find a restroom.

Somehow we're all struggling human heaters in the icy caress
          of straight-backed chairs
even straight-spined backs recoil from,
          and something gets crushed
by too much clarity, like whiting-out the margins
          of our lives
where we probably do most of our living.
          We wake each day
without terms, our thoughts like protostars
          needing their clouds
to fuse. So for next time, don't read the text
          for at least 24 hours
before you write because there's something to be said
          for an emptying of mind
and its thirst for the spirit of the fountain.

With your freewrites fluttering in the early wind
          of dream's undertow,
take a look down those endless corridors
          of letters to come
to at least touch what it is, you somehow
          already know.

A December Morning Decision

Upleaping intruders, two squirrels
in my torpor over coffee,
6 am, and they can capriole
from the tangled, branched dark.
They set their trembling brazenness
on a slit of light at my sill
and wait their due in the pose of monks.
They flick their fanned tails
close over their backs
and their hairs align
under the northwind's magnet.
I lumber to them with a fistful
of nuts and raisins and annoyance
at having to move myself at all.
Across the arcane iced glass,
nose to nose
with the winsome, white-tufted one,
my favorite, whose unmatched feats include
vaulting off with two peanuts at once—
shoves the first way back in his mouth,
with the second's snap just under the teeth—
and shimmying up the birdfeeder pole
to rout out the sunflower seeds.
Looking in, he lingers on the sill
and over his peanuts, splitting them,
leisurely, as if he had earned them,
while I, looking out, resolve to linger
over this coffee, and over this day,
accepting all its offerings,
and to feel entitled to them.

Overlay: On the Spur

To the horses, frothy horses, breaking
into rainbow hooves, raging, leaping
capriciously therefrom the dipper,

he spreads his viridian wave wherever
he pleases. "Hell, can't wait
till I'm good

to start!" He takes one by the tail,
lets it drag him, drenching tangled sable
hairs in his fingers in the plunge

through whitecaps, churning his pigments
up from his undercoat, up for air,
sunsprayed rose madder

genuine, alizarin crimson watereyes.
Some foals squeeze out premature from his tube
to die albinos before the wind.

Uncharted hues gurgle suggestions of hide
he hardly recognizes—even his cankery coat
streaks out before him vague and charging.

"So what if my sky looks coarse,
hell, my colors not translucent enough
for horses galloping foam.

It's the wind, that restless old wind that surfs
on wind that matters—the rainbow's busted flank-
bone be damned!"

Warrior Fire

Out of an ancient savage battle cry
when the drum on the deathbed beat,
and a withered, sapped woman rose
restored in otter skin and shaman beads
on her own two feet, the smokeless pulsation
like laughter loosening a long forgotten peace,

Out of the bilious air deep with conception
when dawn toppled the world splashing within,
and a swollen, queasy woman rose,
soothed despite an emetic drug given
under false pretense of a soother, the researcher awed
at the graph of her faith monitoring her intragastric balloon,

Out of a 2000-year-old crowd moored to marvel and misery
when bleeding footsoles left after-imagery in history
the way suffering became hieroglyphic legend, and a woman
afflicted with uterine bleeding felt the sacred sway
of warrior fire in the flaring garment hem around the legs
of Jesus, instantly healed herself, and began to pray,

Out of the steel in a small boy's hand in North Dakota
when his love levitated a 2-ton car like a spark
floating over his campfire, and his dad trapped beneath the car
was impossibly freed, the investigative team making a chart
to deconstruct the 65-pound, 9-year-old matrix into small,
measurable units defying laws of pulley, lever and lark,

Out of icy thin air poised on a still precipice in Tibbet
when uncanny human generators made heat, with spiritual intent,
and bare yogis wrapped in wet sheets, breathing in, breathing
out, liberated calories within the mindbody crucible most ancient,
the cells like believers dancing round their fires,
in the sheet drying contest that embraced the bitter elements,

Out of the story dragon's habitual fierce breath
when fear first encaved fire to worship reality there,
and a boy paralyzed by polio envisioned a far window, with mind
bellows rocking him toward it while strapped in his rocking chair,
till the window took the fire of the dragon out to the sun,
and Milt Erickson redirected his legs to walk into his frontier,

Out of the "unthinkable impossible" in 50 worldwide journals
when the iconoclast Bannister ran a sub-4-minute mile,
and next year 50 proselytes ran in his offlimits hot tracks,
and the tracks were as hot on illusion's voltaic pile,
when the real was irrelevant to 1/3 the women dosed in placebos,
not chemotherapy, who shed their healthy hair to faith's guile,

Out of the dazzling vitality of the AIDS-infected man
for 9 years symptom-free, the scientific fishing expedition
seeking some unidentified chemical factor in his blood,
out of the shrunken tumor of the NY culinary historian,
who saw red and resisted the doctor's knife-happy response,
out of the valley of the shadow of death, the arcane procession,

Out of the dark frame like medieval paintings we carry
migraine, we carry insomnia, hatred and heart disease,
we carry chronic pain, high blood pressure and anger,
dancers with seizures, executives with allergies,
astronauts with success, an old man with cancer, a young
man with multiple personalities, diabetic in just one of these,

Out of the eyes' opaline calm, the centering
and focusing that reframes the tyrant's storm-wind
into a blustery wail for love, or aplomb's
balance trainer on an ocean-wide reflection,
we primitives of peace quest the way to light,
that masterful outlook within, while raised on the skin,

Out of sheer suggestion, a blister appears
when another subject is touched with the "hot iron"
pencil of the hypnotist, and we quest the way
with aerobic exercise, special diet, abdominal breathing,
we flash cars and missiles, we light candles and rockets,
we stick our skin with needles to illumine,

Out of the endless iconic spinnings, a mindful stillness may come
when cool fire washes the body clean, when cool fire sends
a rippling forgiveness, an overflowing of neuropeptide pools
in channeled healing, aware the earth ignites in fruit
after heavy rain, aware the *Om* is whispering the *Word* is
whispering fiery warrior made graceful within, the pain waxed tame.

Salvation: Recovery Room

And you know,
　all around, yes
　　the air may be breached
　　　again, and it's unbelievable
　　　how some original child
nuzzles just under the skin
　like joy surging in morning's
　　golden-rayed myth.
　　　There is the tonnage
　　　like the afterbirth of desire.
A dream omphalos mocks the fist
　fed with tears—god, is it you?—
　　O, the hunchback side of the heart,
　　the crash unheavenward.
　　　All the marigolds are blue
and each one is someone capped
　in charge of you, whoever you are.
　　Moaning rises and dives and rises
　　　and dives in the darkest loam
　　　that is human all around,
and you know, yes,
　if you could just leap, just
　　leap through that surface, that
　　　is the body that nobody owns,
　　　if you could just glimpse, just
once, what alien intimate tongue
　is pummeling its way upward,
　　through its own stagnant swampland
　　　drowning in sighs
　　　through quicksandy memory

to illusory rockbed,
   if you could just carry your tonnage
     all that way that you could touch
       where someone begins
         moaning, beside you.

From *Shorehaven*

A Perennial Summer Pulse

Its human spirits gone, a place is just
a pile of bricks and sticks and loosely
flying gum wrappers wreathing our sense
of departure, diaspora? Deconstruction
has begun for the new townhouse condominiums
on our years of membership in a Bronx beach club,
where I belonged with my parents and friends,
their parents, sisters, brothers, uncles, aunts,
my childhood sweetheart I married, and our son,
where first I was six, then so was he—
Shorehaven—charged sunspot in my heart,
where my foot first arched into dance,
my arms heaved balls to the hone of craft,
where the wayward wanton of my young energy
first streamed into notebooks like secret woods,
where I undressed from wintry defenses, unlockered
in a thin, silken suit, its ties opening
toward the spinning radiance of love and care,
where I rocked my baby with my sister's, saw them
swim out to the raft of their own small selves,
Shorehaven, where our parents were young and whole.
And though the defiantly enduring human connections
that would outlast this place are few,
and it's true, we do say good-by, we do,
there's a single summer window forever
opening to the record warm, a heat-quivering
place we look across to remember who we are,
how we carry not just a stark field's
frozen woes like an Ethan Frome, we carry
our summer progeny all the way home.

Your Spot

At the beach club you had yours, or you thought
you did. To be sure, you arrived early to haul
the heavy, high-backed, splintery wood-slatted

chairs still unclaimed, that struck like roused
snakes in the grass with their biting slivers.
Scratching and screeching a flagrant trail of yours

alone along the flag stone, or flattening the pliant
grass with your journey lines, your wake resembled
an ancient path across an arcane ritual ground,

your crossings criss-crossing with others from all
the generations that crossed, gathered, and set up
camp here, from a world of ever-moving, impermanent

spots—mom from her 4th bookkeeping job in a year
promotions were landed by men, dad from his night-
shifted day at the post office, my sister from her

5th one-and-only summer beau, and me from my latest
revision of my life—ballerina scratched house painter
scratched savior from religion, with the communists

on the move in my copy of Marx and Vietnam, scratched—
All heaving the heavy chairs, in a Rashomon of lines,
toward that one special spot you could count on,

you thought, to relax in—like Lou Jacobs, the cabbie,
who set up with his family in the field house shade,
while Joe Krinsky set up with his in the abutting

sun patch between the pines, each conspicuously
displaying bridge table and basket, racquets
and blanket, as signs of possession and boundary

of one's piece of the what-never-moved. Then they'd
squabble over whatever wouldn't sit still, like
the sun and the shade and the kids' muddy feet—

All heaving toward something perhaps more elevated
eyes could see, say those on the sundeck, working
on their tans, or making out on blankets, or sleeping

in their spots. But under your particular sycamore,
on your isthmus of cement between the salt water pool
and the fresh water fountain, your strip of grit

behind the bandstand, your half of redwood picnic
table and swath of blacktop in the barbecue area,
your patch of place before the ladies bathroom,

your outskirt's slit of outback overlooking the Sound,
wherever that magnetic memory in your blood trekked
you to, whatever outpost or power pole in turf

or tarmac, so utterly sweet could charm you back
to your very spot you need not prove yourself
worthy to keep, especially on weekends, or after

work, or on a week's vacation, on earth unearned
and unconditionally yours, each time you or a clansman
staked it out early enough by marking each chair,

each ambit of gravel or grass with something of you,
your sweat socks and sneakers, sweatshirts and robes,
your Scotch cooler of chickens, bologna and pickles

in heroes, the scent of your sweat and your food
as distinctive as the musk of a street cat, caught up
by a wind, rising to elaborate the identity of you.

After His Swim

Out of the water, he's dripping,
liquidly, he's sliding down
into his elemental, horizontal
lounge chair, ah!, out in the sun,
suspended as the sundeck in a moire
over there, woven with sultry air,
a deliciously deepening meaninglessness
spreading through his thickening thighs,
with the arcane exhalations
of the work-weary dozers in sunshine,
his fallow skin sun-folding, sun-
breathing, sun-believing, he levels out
to the lemon yellow, yawning will,
his basic matters and antimatters
laid to rest with God and perfect love,
no, not any more, he doesn't
believe in any monkey business
about evolving toward perfection,
not while seeing the world revolving
around fast sports cars and fast bucks,
he doesn't believe the Russians
or Chinese know any better, no,
not the UFO cruisers, nor out-of-body
or commune cultists, but O my god!
he believes, he believes, it's just
free-floating like a ramp in sunshine,
and he doesn't even know what
to do with it any better, but
anointed in ointment, out here—ah!
he doesn't even want the radio on.

The Beating Crossbreed

> On a blanket behind the bandstand,
> our teenage enclave enclosed
> by bushes, the sweet privet's
>
> pollen in our lungs, a wailing
> radio was our hearts' faithful
> metronome, as we did
>
> the bop to *Bye Bye Love,*
> and the Everly Brothers torched
> achings we could cherish,
>
> almost like love. We were snug
> and smug in our new longings
> to overtake the undercurrent
>
> of the waltz from the bandstand
> as our parents were doing their dance,
> two-three, behind us. So we
>
> turned up our volume, to outspin
> them with our fast-moving beat,
> so *Johnnie is a bird dog*
>
> stormed through *que sera.*
> Listening back, I wonder who'd hear
> in such commotions in the winds
>
> how sheaths of music shook loose
> their notes to float like grains
> of pollen, cross-fertilizing

our different currents in the air,
so whatever entered our ears
was never our own pure wail,

but some throbbing crossbreed
of the generations' melodies,
underneath a purling sun.

Picnic

We feasted in the open air, where apples
should be crunched, right through the skin and seeds,
beneath a basting sun that reddened our cheeks,
the sweet juice of tidbits running through our lips
with our own ripening, in the savor of place,
kindled by mom's chickens and singing off-key,
high-strung notes that much was known and eased
in the faces leaning in on our consuming table.
Her abstract wish to be generous came out
in food, new red potatoes and Spanish rice,
tree-tossed greens and baby Brussel sprouts.
Even the ribs at each other sucked out
to the marrow, no leftovers but years, intertwining
within that meal's vast, unknowing spout.

Sunbather

You look like a schwartze! was a compliment,
the blacker the better, the richer the skin,
the more convincing leisure's illusion,
though blacks were not allowed in.
Each summer in advance of next summer,
members knew to pay, so Doc, the owner
of the beach club could say, *Sorry,
we're all full this season.* Earning
the blackness on your back was the difference.
And around the pool on cement blocks,
women crushed their breasts doing backs,
while their children worked in their coloring books.
The sundecked writhed and turned as if
on a spit of sacrifice for color for which they burned.
Grass baskers could feel how the soul seemed to soar
a little higher from the surface of the skin.
Sweating out their vacations, hardball players
darkened around their leather gloves, went back
to work embarrassed by their lilyish hands,
or to their two-week calls to the colors
on Nam-safe, National Guard bivouacs,
where they practiced race riot control.
Even unhatted at the outdoor show,
you could distinguish yourself in the audience
by the particular hue you achieved—
bronze being better than red,
and red being better than freckled,
freckled being better than splotchy,
and splotchy being better than peeling,
with all sorts of invidious in-betweens,
like how golden the tiniest hairs' sheen

on the arms, how colorfast the roots
on the head. *Oh I hate you! You don't
even have a difference under there!*
Whiting-out their lips and ears,
or blacking out their eyes with plasti-shades,
to be on the safe side in the color phase
of the year was common, long before
carcinogens and electron-positron colliders
were in, when the z's in the air were just
as uncaptured, just as arcane in the gusty
exhalations of the work-weary dozers
in sunshine, whose everyday matters and antimatters
never rested, even off from work as they
worked on their tans. And then the flaking
down to one's true colors was just
as inevitable, while the colors were raised
on proud white poles everyday,
and the other color guard worked the gate.

Summer Rain

Rain took us

  by surprise

    in the heat
      of our bodies,

in the beat
  of active purpose:
    a racquet about to swing,
      a burger about to fling,

a conjuring in a lounge chair
  about to assume its dais dream.
    It gathered us like so many
      human drops running

our scattered belongings
  under a common shed,
    an open overhead, no walls,
      all our eyes focusing
        on the same flashing,
          hard, driving, demanding
            rain, rain, rain, rain.

Flattened bouffants clung
  to our elemental faces,
    freed of make-up. We
      wrapped our wetselves
        in cozy blankets,
          the great equalizers
            of old powwows on this spot,

levelling snazzy bows and hues
  on our bathing suits and trunks,
    priming us to chew the fat
      as we huddled at, against,
        across the redwood tables.
          We shared fruit and stories,
            our leftover tidbits,

whatever there was.
  The press of the flesh
    was hamish and homey
      in our storm's open house
        with overhead dripping,
          the wood beams deepening,
            steeping into original fragrance.

Our rain-ripened voices, musty
  and rich, wistful and whimsical,
    wisecracking into wise,
      our eyes like safe doors,
        flung open, the private goods
          revealed, as if we were delivering

ourselves to each other
    for the first time,
      our directional sense
        foggy, each wet, woken

voice coming in clearer, closer,
    as if we could keep on,
      adrift on an ark

of renewing

rain.

Nets

Summer was not official until the nets were raised,
like Old Glory over our heads on the volleyball courts,
stretched and spined across the tennis greens,
hitched to wave and droop from basketball hoops,

draped across the ping-pong tables, colorfully
restored like hope at the outset of each endeavor
to grapple against the squash walls. We raised the nets
so we could defy them without pulling them down.

Net ball! Do over. You touched the net! You're out!
You were over the net! Under the net! Yanked the net!
You're out! You're out! You're out! Net tenets
all knots sometimes, but sometimes all air,

where you found yourself moving through. For nets
cast shadows full of holes that caught the sun
of our striving. A laying on of hands for a swift-
skimming slam just atop the volleyball net,

or sometimes a smooth swish without hoop or backboard
ckabock! untoeing the line, or nearly sweeping
against the abrasive floor with your belly,
and you'd find a door for the joyous animal

that was pacing within its stall. Places of change,
mystic membranes of our stretching thresholds
toward a knowing beyond our reach. How good
to overtake our height, to ascend long-legged,

long-armed, to feel the whole rising day
pouring into our lungs, some granite hunk chunked
off from the gravity of our lives, Ariel's easy
motion aloft and independent of body. Here

where it was all between you and the net, and it
always would be, where our winning and losing sides
got delineated, our inept, inconstant, timid-handed,
and our adept, cocky, sure-footed sides could

see themselves in each other through the holes
in ourselves, if we dared look, while *Your feet drop
anchor in the asphalt!* sailed back and forth…
We loved our nets, their magnanimous lets,

the erratic skips the ball like a heartbeat made
off the rim, tipped into granting a second chance.
Women wore them with sparkles in their hair
to wink as the stars of their striving at the dance

on Saturday nights, or they did themselves out
in fishnet stockings to catch transcendence,
often left with nettled legs. Outdoing herself
and Moishe's in a fishnet bag, mom packed

her homeground liver, her secret airiness,
a few Ritz crackers. We netted our lifelines out
on graph paper, studying for finals in June,
our scribbles what we caught in our looseleafs

from immense fleets of words with our clumsy nets
of understanding. Sprawled across the blanket
and each other in our shifting friendship network,
we read our fishy shadows of Plato, Melville, Bio.

Let there be A's in those boxes! Let there be
a white veil between us! me and my basketball star-
accountant, a switch-hitter of net swishes
and net worth. And when we cast our mosquito nets

across Paul's carriage, *Let there be light*
but no stinger strong enough to tear that net,
nor small enough to slip through! I prayed
to the sieve of the universe, under the sycamores,

their leafy nets so fine they could enmesh the sun
and keep their game going over our heads
all summerlong, as they did long ago, over the heads
of the Indian fishermen chanting *Let there be*

fish and favor by the spirits! as they cast out
their nets on the Sound, on this very ground
of our Shorehaven, where shared nets of knowing
caught us and knit us together to this place.

The Field House

Opening early, under a sky already ardent with orange,
the field house drew us, through air ripply with summer
energy before our very eyes. We rushed to it

from all directions, with our passes and hot hanker
to heave balls through hoops, slice back bouncers
at apt angles, rev up gut racquets, rocket disks

down slim-laned alleys, where we always knew the score.
A white-washed, open hut on the grass, air in its
baskets of basketballs, drawn from that grass

and pulled from the pines, got pumped through the balls
and into our lungs. So insides were like outsides, like
grass and pines, like sky, if we'd thought all

about it, but we didn't, just stamped around till called
by Mr. Welson, the athletic director with a bad back
girdled. He took our passes, propelled us with paddles

and ping-pong balls, volleyballs, and buckets stacked
with disks, shuffleboard sticks, basketballs and black
hard balls, and we went from the field house to fields

of unslanting light, with energy fields aching in our limbs
for definition: server, receiver, or somebody's guard,
somebody's partner at a sweetsharp edge motion yields.

Eddy

While the Merlin of memory youthens him
now that I've gotten older, I see
I got careless and caught his age somehow.
But way back then, the white whammy

already was streaking his hair much older
than we ponied girls. At the club he was
our volleyball wizard who'd sleight the net
that hobbled our shots as it towered above us.

He was a teacher by trade and temperament,
whose green eye cusps held summer
like an alchemy of a whole wide time
to get children to learn the art of whatever.

Who'd ever forget his green driven gaze
to get us to raise our inept, bolting balls,
up over the net, out beyond ourselves…
His determination slipcased a collection of skills

his rigid back lacked what it took
to use. As he coaxed and coached the loose
abracadabra in our young spines,
he couldn't do half of what he knew

to do, like dive to save one dying
on the net, or vault up in sky to
spike wildfire. Yet he set us diving
down to the blacktop, down close to view

time scraping from the skin of our knees—
The way recouping rabbit feet leap
back from black hats, after their bodies
disappeared, suspending gravity with disbelief,

we'd spring the ball and ourselves back up
and—Presto!—New life off the net!
Each day, Eddy just appeared to us
whenever it was our turn for the court.

He showed us our strength in fingers together,
to craft a serve, the hand must heel,
the eye observe the heft of weather,
and the holes of opportunity to steal

into on the other side, how the height
of high nets could be surmounted,
drilled down by practice… practice…
of angles to net in the body attitude.

He worked the wind into our swing,
helped remove the weights from our feet.
Eddy knew true leisure was work
put to love in full summer heat.

How many Eddies have come into my life
and left some wizardry without a trace,
how many Eddies can I even recognize
in the sleight of the moment, face to face?

Twenty-One

I had a sustained courtship
with basketball. For 25 summers
twenty-one was our game.
Singles or doubles, midday,
amid fresh air and friends,
hotfooting after rebounds
to shoot back on the spot,
sinkers earning foul shots.
Rocketed rebounds commandeered
the catcher to remote positions,
where long one-handers
made miracles, or air balls
that got *your ass to the brass!*
for pole-shot hooks, up
at the hooped sun, a blind
heave—swished—or smashed
the cocky from your head.
On good days, the basketball
was the globe in my hands,
steered by latitude seamlines,
the backboard resonating
from my fingers' hot tips,
sweat pouring me into the trees,
oxygen filling me with some
holy ghost of motion,
the ball flying me through
some hiatus in the chain
of limits on the chine, some
days some pure deliverance,
the backboard and hoop untouched,

the ball a leathery third eye
seeing clear through to gamesoul.
At 20 points, the climactic,
dizzying, two-handed backshot,
the over-the-head sight,
the body arched back, up
over the whole wide upside,
giddy with wild possibility.

Foul Shooting

I

Just once in my life
I hooped 19 out of 20
foul shots, in training
under myself to outdo myself.
I turned the seams to verticals
so the ball streamlined.
With belief I drilled
as the hoop expanded
to fill my vision's circle.
I aimed at an imaginary
ball arching toward
a private channel
practice deep-carved
in the air. I breathed better
doing what I loved.
And I began to sense,
as the ball left my hands,
when its message delivered
would be the message heard
—an off-the-backboard sinker—
or when its message in transference
would be without a sound
—a spirited swish—
without touching the rim.
In the spring of my body,
the drive with right hand,
as hoop-hand distance shrank,
sometimes a release clicked
technical to spiritual,

and the ball was my extension
into flight in split seconds
with my feet aloft from earth—
the ball my tear through
its womb of gravity,
and I was born to air,
the ball my Icarus,
my solo crossing,
time capsule, sun probe.
In dissolving to motion,
my blood coursing
in vessels to legend,
my ball swelling to myth,
each planted basket
was a seed into confidence,
an airy, obscure presence
inside the nets of me.

II

That once in my life
was not at the tournament
for women's foul shooting,
when my feet fouled me
3 times—jumped the line,
put the kibosh on 3
of my swishes, so I lost,
or won, depending
if shadow or light
overtook the bronze ball
on my 2nd place trophy.

If bronze was cast in light,
some stubborn kernel woke
as inside a winged seed
inside me to grow, sprawl
branches, extend outside.
If bronze was cast in shadow,
some vague dissatisfaction—
as when leaving home,
that sense something important
has been left undone,
what keeps us forever trying
to get back there—
which kept asking me what
propelled that underhand drive
under the tournamented ball
under myself to outdo the best,
the feeling less than most?
I like to think
the last homecoming hoop
awaits me to swish through
to a trophyless place,
where there are no foul shots
against the self,
no title to defend,
no defense needed
to be entitled.

How I Met My Husband

(for Mike)

So much depends upon
a white bread sandwich
glazed with noon sunshine,
beside the net stitchings
of a basketball court,
where a boy, keeping
time with a ball and with
the man he would be,
is watching the girl on the grass
holding the sandwich, on that
so much depends, not just
a garden's redwood bridge
beside a house, not just
unforeseen flecks of hazel
sandwiched between the brown
in a baby's eyes, so much,
that the girl alone, on a blanket,
distracted by the blond boy,
just cannot grasp all
of its contents, so hearty
its load, it's seeping onto
her fingers, glazing them
sticky, beside the bandstand,
More than the greatest love…
stitching into the secret scales
in the girl's mind, untuned
to the woman she would be,
who never would get a hold
on all ingredients, ever

so slowly it all digests,
the boy coming from the court
to her on the blanket, his line
all glazed, *Hi, I think
I know you, we must
have met before sometime.*

       Shorehaven Beach Club
       The Bronx, 1959

The Escape Artist Was Up

Dad was up—back bent—knees bent
gave a bounce to a hard black re-
active ball—Whack!—his serve low
oblique—it whomped off the wall—
Atta boy, Ruby! his partner Lefty
cracked—snapped into position
from the sideline—the rebound
swept just past the short line—
one opponent dove—gloved hand'n
knee catching concrete—just skinned
it underhand—*Shit!*—a high-bounder
on the wall wafting time to Dad—
he walloped it on a fly—placed it
low—the volley was on—fire-paced
fast-angled thwacks—making black
tracks on the white-washed wall
—controlled low ball fusillades—
whop—whap—swap-swop—legs'n
arms darted to targets—minds molded
to a ball in the air—where time
belonged—untouching anything con-
crete—unmaking human friction
where Dad slid-swivelled-swat open
his space inside the certain sound
the ball makes—its plea—im-
possibility!—I watched him play out
his heart as if he could keep it
up forever—on split-slam time—
KILLER!..

Great shot Baby! slapped to Dad's back
by Lefty—*Just shielding my jewels!*
And the ball bounced off my glove!—
Dad tossed it away with a low re-
active laugh—and in his afterglow
in his orange boxer shorts with sun
glistening on his sweat—salt teasing
out his tan—his whole body remembered
radiant and breathing the depths—
Mom's fear burst from behind the fence
where spectators had gathered to watch
a game of best players on the 1st court
—*Ruby! That's enough!*—threatening him
with *Heart attack! You want a heart*
attack like Schneider! Heart attack!
springing onto his court in her faded
tiger suit—springing at its walls'
capacity to seal him from her
within life or death—she wanted him
by her side at the 4 o'clock show
—*Hilda! You want to embarrass me*
in front of the guys? he rebounded—
The guys laughed.........................

I watched him walk off the court
with her—his back bent as if ready
to serve—the guys snickering—re-
shuffling positions—and one day
when I wasn't there he would walk off
the court for good—the sedentary
palsied Parkinson alien already taking
stooped possession of his court—
parblind and spoon-fed by my mother
with a pacemaker box bulging through
his chest like some live memento
handball court connected to his heart
—pretending sleep when she was chatty—
He was an escape artist—and that day
he found his way out through her sleep
—back to work within the walls
he loved—back to what his day off
was really all about—back out
to the handball court—and I was
an escape artist's daughter—I
never told—not all—not even now—
but there he is in his leather gloves
swinging with both hands—fast-placing
the ball where no one is looking……….

Off the High Board

Out to that far raft, I pushed,
on and on, puffing and
panting in endless approach,
to thrust my whole weight on-
to the slippery island of self-
testers, to climb up and
up again, the pool's longest,
slipperiest ladder because
I staked my fear up there,
where the wildly whistling
wind woke a concentrated
saltiness upon my skin,
and it would be fun, then, to
dare the dark plunge
while it was still light,
the same dark plunging
stakes into beauty's heart
in the long drop of my hands
from my eyes, when double-dared
by a friend to look directly
at the killer, while I stood
all alone in that movie aisle,
so I would walk the plank
again, alone out there,
poised on an inner hush
I must have known as
the beautiful quiet when my
heart first dove into its living
waters, up where all the
shimmering of summer's pool

was pulling together into my
waterglass to fill with me,
a Tarzanian daredevil, fast-
falling on a solid rope
of time—a moment's rimless
light—all stars!—on impact,
a cold, shattering crash,
falling as far down as
I was high, the pressure
up my nose, in my lungs,
and the water was humming,
its dissolved presences alive
and daring me, don't rise, not
a moment too soon, to keep
my eyes open, and scrape
along the bottom's Atlantis
by the central sucking drain,
to touch it, and torpedo up
through that broad inner smile
when the master beast of being
feels fed. But many slick
and subtle ladders later,
there are days wrung through
that once when I was about
to spring out from my plank
over the rest of my years,
and saw the awful height of fear
up there, and I turned around,
climbed down the high board ladder,
and never went up it again.

Bathing Suit

                    Shucked off at season's end,
                  summer's second skin,
                 fabric and flesh passing
                into each other, the belly's
              loosened elastic a flaccid
          placid sybarite, the fibers
of consequence bleached,

                     salted, sun-stunned to wan.
                  How naked can you get
                and still keep covered,
              the original challenge,
          like a poetry of tummies
       tucked behind the thin,
illusive, diagonal lines.

                    Full-skirted thighs flapped
                 about in windy gossip,
               loosely midriffed layers of
             appetite comically ballooned
          in the see-through-all pool,
       where a foam-solid, bobbing
mermaid boob went

                    floating off each now and
                 then, an unclaimed breast
               of how your body will
             betray you, down to
          your first bathing suit.
       Get a tiger by the tale a
squeezed cleavage told,

a few stripes to a tawny coat
and her frailest yellow was hidden
from most who went by suits, but
dad and me, who'd seen mom,
her buff trembling. I remember
long lines at Alexander's, hours
we riffled through racks

once suits went skimpy, for
the more undressed, the more
responsible each strip
to form the floating mask.
Long before I saw my friends,
I learned to spot their suits.
But most suits are unsuitable

to nature's changing contours,
each stretch leaving scars
peek-a-booing from hiding,
as birthmarks on kids and moms
from their long swim together—
kicking out from one suit, parting
to learn the waterways.

After Paul was born, I shucked
the panoplied suit for a bikini,
proud to be marked with stretch.
Today I tried on an old suit,
felt its telltale flesh-cling,
its palpable push toward
a nude swim in radiance.

Poolside Seduction

My ladder is slick with your residue Slide into me I'll hold you high
high as you trust Come closer I can get through your woven suit
I'm cool I'll slip inside the tucks of your yearning I'll wash your
greasy grimy creases as you fold your body inside your mind I'll
pour myself inside your ears hear your heart beating its inattentions
malcontents I'll buoy your floating life fortune's bobbing friends and
family I'll lap your bleeding wounds caught on time's fishhooks
Through me see you There There A glimmering shifting motion A
recollection of reflections I'll sound your lungs filling with gasp Lap
Lap Trust me Open your eyes Keep under See people dangling
overhead features flaring like out of science fiction LapLap I'll
release your time capsules   Burst open your bubble voices
LapLapDissolve Your father's unflappable hand holding your belly
as you learn your tread Lap Lap The thrash of your young son's thighs
his pudgy plashing playful thighs SlapSlap Kick me Kick me No
matter I keep no marks Come leap for each other in meYour memory
lapse doing its flapdoodle laps LapLapDissolve LapLap Your pal
Diane Blood sister Your pinpricking oath dripping red in me deep
sixing your charms Champ swimmer doing her overlaps through
thunderclaps Determined to keep you in me all day You can't keep
up There There Kick me hard   as you can   I'll tell you the same
scintillating scattering truth Lap Lap Either everything or nothing
shimmering matters LapLapDissolve Count every stroke your father
said Keep kicking   I'll float your broken metaphor mirrors back
Your skin is my putty to pucker   I'll float your claptrap bubbles of
waste   and want   back in slicked rainbow sheen Push off that firm
floor Let my ripply rhythm lift you   Feel you not even having to
hold on Did you think that man could keep you up   Did that boy
think it was you   You cried as he thrashed swallowed me all his
way out Listen fool flapper You can't swim here Sentinels of endless
summer are gone What's keeping you up Look down I'm drained

Summer's Seasoning

Salt on our legs
   like a shoreline
   is ambling its clinging
bone rime
   from our salty pool
   fed by the Sound
and the sounds of people
   in motions bound
   with thirst for life
and we carry its burning
   a concentration like love
   in sweat and tears as
one salt tracing
   as human sea rim
   itching to deepen us
from our long swim
   together in spite
   of ourselves our fears
into each other's skin
   as we linger
   suspended in sunshine
in the pause between
   ticks in the wings
   of time when
we dissolve within
   this spice of life
   that can heal old wounds
but won't brush off.

Diamonds and A Girl's Best Friend

Do I have diamonds between my legs?
I'd never thought to ask before
that contest taught me applied

geometry. *Put your knees and ankles*
together, Mom nudged. *You're supposed*
to have three. That's what she'd heard—

One between the thighs, in there,
one between the knees and calves,
and one between the calves and ankles.

I pushed, protracted my balking legs.
One semi-precious diamond scored
my thighs. One cramped muscle complained.

One long neck of a goose, I filliped,
was caught up to my knees. But I
was *still developing,* Mom consoled.

Till showdown time, Diane and I
watched guys swing out their hearts
on the belly-whopped baseball diamond,

then chased after ourselves to the stage,
where contest preparations had been made—
a fabric bolt rolled out as wall

above leg height for foiling faces
and identifying traits to judge
the women justly just by legs.

We practiced forcing diamonds
with pressure, patting, sympathetic pinching,
whatever it took to strangle the goose

between the calves. Diane squeezed
out a four-diamond miracle.
I relearned how to walk stiff-kneed.

With Diane my cane, my legs transformed
spasmodically to gems in the rough.
Relieved to sit down with my buddy,

I felt the gems revert to goose.
And we applauded the parade of shaved,
Naired, waxed, unpolished gems.

Front. Side. Veiny-back view.
The nicked, wobbly, lopsided, chunky,
sinuous, bodiless, Betty Grable-

 contoured, headless, high-scored legs,
spiked and caught like fish in nets,
ahead of us on stage, for what

we took as women, raising whistles
and *Attababy! Attababy!*
We kept applauding. Semifinalists.

The finalists. And finally,
we got up and joined in cheer—
Miss Shorehaven Legs 1958!!!

And then we clapped our hands around
each other's perfect fit, and skipped,
and dove like fish into the pool's crowd.

A Girl/ A Woman

I sit next to a girl and watch her
watching the woman in a skin-tight
suit stepping into the cardboard
cutout in the hourglass figure
of Diana Dors upon the stage.
I want to warn the girl so
rapt in the hourglass, I
can   cut out some turns
for   her   in   there, as
she watches a woman
whose hips just
will not fit—
there's the
rub/ bruised
blush as out-
line of model
shape scrapes skin
from the woman emerg-
ing with her distorted
smile. I want to warn the
girl, who keeps a cardboard
box of paper dolls in a closet
—each doll cut out along dotted
lines, tabs folded on prefab poses—
as the next woman thrusts her breasts
out to the frame like plush pile to home

tacking—I want to warn the girl
watching the woman who fits so well
she could get stuck in there. She's
so young, young enough to be my
daughter, as she watches a man
wrap a tape measure around
the waist of a scored woman
to announce how form-
fitted her 24 I want
to warn the girl
that the show's
a trickling
instrument
of sandy
kisses/ shell
prizes, how cut-
outs hold airheads,
but how can she hear me,
she's so preoccupied with
the hot-pink bathing suit
my mother got her for her
birthday, with her first kiss
flush on her lips under the sun-
deck last night, and years of turning
the hourglass until she lets me into
her frame with the substance of love.

Harry Bruce

Harry Bruce weighed three-fifteen.
Short-armed, bald, he heaved his wheeze
     walking to the stone fountain for a drink.

But when he dove, like a seal out to sea,
deep in dance, *Cherry Pink and Apple Blossom*
     with Ann, as Harry twirled, he streamlined,

sleek motion immersing him in time.
Eyes on eyes, spins succinctly clipped,
     hips swished through current's floating dip.

Harry Bruce dared bliss with his body,
a body many spurned. He could
     loosen illusions with a glide-sway-turn,

cha-cha-cha. We burned,
anchored to our feet, to execute
     the pachanga-merengue-peabody-mambo

feats of Harry Bruce. We burned
for passion's proportion on a hot, cement
     dance floor, 2pm, under stagnant sun.

Tuesdays, Thursdays, two rows facing Harry,
trying to mirror his way, the way
     water mirrors the land's solid moves

to fluency, like poetry, Harry, head erect,
the music sliding in-between-his-bones.
     His ease the center of our lesson,

as dripping sweat beneath our bathing suits,
we tried to toe, two-three,
        the cool element of Harry Bruce.

        Even that summer he lost a hundred pounds,
donned a belt and a trim toupee,
        in dance, he remained fully his own.

        Thanks Harry, wherever you are,
for the selfless joy you rippled to me,
        a girl grown up on your cha-cha line,

        for elegance spinning through a wide-rib cage,
thanks Harry, wherever you are,
        for the largeness of grace in a shimmy's sheer shape.

The Saturday Night Dance

Call for summer, starry evening,
the long, lingering lingo of sax
seductively snaking through dancers in the dark,
in the humid air drenched with desire.

The long, lingering lingo of sax
is music's hedonist arm around waist,
in the humid air drenched with desire,
bending and pressing a heart to a heart.

In music's hedonist arm around waist,
a sustained note of what we've lost,
bending and pressing a heart to a heart,
beating the unceasing need to keep

a sustained note of what we've lost.
The stage has headlights into tomorrow,
beating the unceasing need to keep,
as dips rhyme hips into fingertips.

The stage has headlights into tomorrow:
Shoulders shrug off—what's older?—
as dips rhyme hips into fingertips,
and love's lascivious timing sways.

Shoulders shrug off—what's older?—
Call for summer, starry evening,
and love's lascivious timing sways,
seductively snaking through dancers in the dark.

The Virginia Reel

Across our evening's warbling
whoop-de-dooing strings,
the fiddlers' fingers are flying,
our rapture is in full swing,
hours into square dancing,
with loose skirts and lungs ballooning,
and long, flying hair outspinning
misery's long overrated wring,
as people are paired, outwheeling
the moon, and couples clasping
couples are whisked to centering
grasps, are rapt in clarifying
touch, these ancient turnings
to tribal song, to outbeating
memory in fired footings
and a slide-sensed holding
another in vibrant intermingling,
this human circle is a way of knowing
how grand union's ring
of right and left, and promenading
on light moon-weight legs,
do-si-doing and honoring
the joy of the flesh in tuning
our flesh to dance-up its living.

Unconditional Return

Rusty bandstand, upon your faint heartbeat,
I lay my head, upon your steady, mute song,
the pulsing music of the flesh comes
purer from far away, on rarefied strings,
like an old mother's love. How I danced
to your ensnaring beat when I was young,
and now your beat keeps dancing within me.

Dilapidated ball courts, upon your dislocated spine,
I rest my sinewy swing, upon your persistent
resounding *Do better! Do better!*
I can! I can! rebounds off walled-in defeat.
I feel the press your racquet left on my lifeline.
Fallen fountains, upon your flattened spirit,
my summer thirst drinks of its life.

Drained swimming pool, upon your dry womb
with seemingly little left to give, I stay
my heart, upon your crusty salt rime
burning wounds open in memory. The day
I nearly drowned, I learned to kick from you,
and now I dream I breathe underwater with faces
you taught me to know swimming through my own.

Our Son's ID Photo Off an Old Pass

In a recess in our closet,
in black and white terms
like a mug shot for a crime,
it hangs, over the tracks
we kept of his getaway growth:

—1/2/86 taller than mom no shoes
—6/3/85 kept up with dad on track
—5/4/79 took off training wheels
—9/9/74 1st day nursery school
—1/9/72 stood self no hands

This two-inch, mighty face,
his ID to a vandalized gate,
abandoned to memory, is doing
time. Within his dark eyes,
there's a rush of white mirth dots,

that laughter is loosening up
his being wheedled into waiting
for the flashy eye to freeze
his lit grin, wispy brow,
wiseacre poise, onto his pass

as little boy, already obsolete
in its frozen moment, as every photo
lies before a developing face.
Announced by a security guard,
we visit him in Washington,

where he's working toward
his doctorate. So proud,
we're embarrassed to admit
our complicity with grandpa,
who, having known how to tummy-

tickle a boy but not talk teen,
scrawled and double-underlined
across the scissored bangs,
the lifetime parole: <u>WANTED.</u>

Sunset Discovery

Full-bellied, squabble-sated,
slack-limbed and on their backs,
no matter how many people
discovered the sunset
and took it in, they never
consumed it. The range of reds
as subtle as the earth's,
the loud lavenders dulled down
to dusk's pastels, the electric
washed out from yellows, blues
white-edged with salt and browned
with sweat, all across the grass
in their chromatic, look-at-me suits
across their naked flesh, blonded
and bronzed in instinctive health,
they made a softened rainbow,
an unconscious rainbow in relinquishment.
It was that certain time of day
when they least saw themselves.

Summer Leaves Resonating

Little silvered tongues
the wind whips up, and
up, in close, concentric
layers of summer, a feeling
for wet footprints, forever
disappearing, into the noisy,
four-leaf clover, salt-
water pool, over the
long years, the salt
of the earth, mind's rime
of path to desert, sprouting
inside us, under a
single rain, refracting
many human hues
as a place we knew, its
music sweeping from the bandstand
out through its grassy fields
and ball fields, seeping
into dim lockers, fixing
voices in fields of energy,
floating translucently through
fluid leaves of being.

From *One Small Kindness*

Moving Day

On Evergreen Avenue, in three little rooms
of a Bronx apartment, with high walls,
stippled with gold leaf in the living
room and roaches in the kitchen, where four fit
into one bedroom, and then where they moved
their adult sleep to the living room convertible,

it began with excitement. The Castro convertible
was rooted out from the rug, as dad shouldered the rooms'
furniture around to the rhythms of mom's moving
visions. He steered chairs by their wings to walls,
where they lit with new-angled sun for months of fit,
their cracked plastic covers breathing as if living,

as we sat in a novel place, facing the living
window world, watching an inverted pail convert
bugs and straw into feathery flyers that fit
their alchemy through slits in our fire escape to rooms
of sky and cloudwalls. Half-opened, the window was a wall
of voices from kitchens and showers and lots with children moving

spokes and sticks, ropes and balls. Our moving
needed no van, just dad, who quietly carried his living,
moving letters and passengers, and mom's wallpaper-
covered cornices, the fireplace that converted
a light bulb's heat to the spokes of a wheel, from room
to room, a harnessed suggestion of fire fitfully

flickering with replenished visage, sweet comfit
for the imagination on moving day. We moved
with mom's seasons, country colors and roominess
transmuting the plaster with our one painting of rustic living.
Each wall got sent to its camp and conversed
with a fresh air. My grandparents moved to stonewall

the rent they couldn't pay. My parents moved to stonewall
the rent they could pay, to stretch to outfit
their lives and their children's lives with meager, convertible
furnishings, like hand-me-downs, the urge to movement,
to free what inhabits cramped walls, a song of living,
like birds that could build in a washbucket's straw rooms.

Now I pencil the Evergreen walls, its moving
light flitting across the infitted figures of living
and loving, converting to sacred shabby furnishings of inherited
                              rooms.

His Harmonica

"Give me a song," he'd say,
  and we'd eagerly oblige,
naming pop tunes like *Tammy,*
  Spanish Eyes, or *Edelweiss.*
Then cradling the little wood frame,
  he'd close his music-blind eyes,
to lip-read the notes as he'd slide
  his mouth along the slotted rows,
blowing and sucking his tidal reeds
  down private wind channels unseen
beneath the flashing steel casing.
  It's Cherry Pink and Apple Blossom White
became his protoplasmic breeze
  that freed the cha-cha in our waking feet.
"Hello again and a great howdy do!"
  the man of few words woke me
and sent me to school fed and keyed
  on his reeds, the one true thing he
could bend to his will, make malleable
  as his mustache tipping its silvery artery,
pumping, pumping, his air-stopping solo…
  "Dad, I'll give you a song," I say,
as he lies trapped inside his life
  like a turtle on its back, his arms waving
and pulling at his socks on his hands that keep
  him from pulling out his tubes
in the valley of the shadow of syncopated memory.

"I'll give you a song," I say,
and place his fingers to feel its voice,
   as his perpetual pump is dripping his food,
his urine bag filling in bloody,
   his paralyzed eyelids are closed, his eyes
shut-ins behind their gargantuan shade.
   Its patient silent passageways play
to him, incapable of speech, animating
   in his dark, a smile of chords striking
in him "My harmonica! My harmonica!"
   He tries to lift it up, and slowly,
like bench-pressing a great weight,
   he gets it to his lips, feebly
blows, stokes up one note,
   one vibrato ember from within his being,
then drops it like a barbell—"It's cherry
   pink," I sing for him, "apple blossom"—

Ulysses and Child

This is not about the somber light
in a hospital room, the slow, steady
falling into deepest evening, nor your
calling for home again. "Okay,
let's go upstairs," you say, and make
for my hand, and for the irretrievable
threshold into your old bedroom
of salmon sheets, a paper Mediterranean
behind the bed, where your realest voyage
you ever made was rising up, and
down, on its silvery springs with mom,
your own bed a distant beauty—
you'll never reach that port again.
This is not about the blood clot
in your leg, the dead muscle they removed,
nor the deep bone chasm beneath the gauze
like sails you hoisted over the guardrails,
your being tied six weeks to the bedpole,
captivated by the sight of home, the nurses
laughing sirens. "What kind of a daughter
are you! Why won't you take me home?"
nor my search for the right words again.
This is not about having to shit
lying down, being diapered by your daughter,
nor not breathing unwalled air four months,
nor, speaking intravenously, when day
assumes the whispering drip of night,
the slow-wheeling into disappearance
of capability after capability—

feeding yourself, walking on your own,
understanding the why and the where of who
you are, this your furthest journey from me.
But this is not about all that.
This is about the rush of first air
that frees the rooted trees, that scampers
the squirrels and the human spirits overhead,
after each other, up and down, and
down, and up again, on their emblazoned masts,
as I push you in the wheelchair outside,
and we pause to smell the falling blossoms
spring remembers so well that I see
my joyously journeying carriage with my baby
the first time we traveled the street
after his birth. A pure, happy moment
is never about journey's end,
but belief in horizon again, and oh!
the gusty, fresh air on the skin.

The Maroon Scrabble Set

has strings now holding it together,
like an old family instrument.
My sister and I played for self-esteem,

laboring in our breathing to deliver ourselves
as best daughter. Grit caught between
the letters of our words as we were marooned

in competition on our beach blanket, enmeshed
in crusts from corners of dreams our
laboring parents learned as living disappointment.

We interlocked our do-re-mi like horns,
used root words against each other,
unknowing then how to build on them.

The strategy, moving in more than one way
at once, taking the advantage with words,
never got us speaking what rattled insecurities,

feeling in the wind nothing was good enough,
the vibrato *What happened to the other point
on the spelling test?* And we sat quietly at dinner

when mom hurt with migraine from harsh words
at work, and the work of more archaic words
scrabbling inside her, outside our reach.

Playing us one against the other,
with an alphabet of her own wounds,
her gameboard scored us, and we competed

for love, pulled language from a dark pouch.
We got good at honing points from the rack
    of wants. By the time we were sophomoric teens,

    we were calling it moral victory for any score
despiting our given hands. Across the board,
    we tiled our crosswords like elaborate sandcastles

    built to be broken, and we sat quietly at dinner.
We accused each other of having all
    the letters—BA MA MRS—

    and still the feeling there was no winning,
only the myriads of scrabbling scurriers
    caught by a churning tide, where our children

    were scribbling their sand notes like fragments
of music to the sea. Who knows how we change?
    Maybe in minding our children, we mind ourselves.

    Maybe as they outletter us with Ph.D,
and our parents minds drift out
    on a sea of lost words, we find humility.

    Maybe it's the years building sand
and spilling out each time we loosen
    the strings around this game the color

    of old blood scar. Maybe it's how
what tenses in our throats with words
    becomes as music all one tense, as in our

pulsing laughter on the rocking pontoon
out on the lake, taking mom into our game,
    helping her play her hand like mothers,

    with pulsing tears over the hospital bed
where dad lay drowning in a sea of tubes,
    speechless, and where a tumor racked me

    for two months, while my sister carried
my daily highlight, our Scrabble game.
    To celebrate this calm day without calamity,

    I tuck the list of vowel dumps
my sister sent like a fret beneath
    the strings of our maroon set, beaming

    my headlights toward the one I'm most tied
by scoreless inner threads, anticipating
    the pleasure achieving each other's winning smiles.

Marriage

At night, in absent light, we reach for each
familiar feel, for each lone cell's soul
in tender touch, and we are all approach—
from thirty-two together years, we hold
a draw as flesh become magnetic as
the gently clasping leaves of our prayer plant,
old hurts tenacious as the mud wasp nests
on frames around our windows, we have kept
on knocking off with sticks, to find them back
again, in some remoter niche, as beneath
his father's old strapping chair—he's hurrahed
for my poems' inspire, as I his aspire as "big brother,"
as face to face, we breathe into countless wee balloons
we hold unseen in our lungs, enabling each chest to rise.

Soufflé for Two

Sometimes we serve it up cold,
scraping lumps and starchy edges
like prison food, our meal like fate,
mostly what we make for each other,
the undone dishes prophetically rimmed
in the grime of our daily fare.

Sometimes we whip up a smoothie,
so sweet to the tongue we can hide
the bitterest things, like ancestral herbs
we sift into kitchen clouds
rising from cup to cup to our lips.

Sometimes it comes out too rich,
we don't dare indulge how much we want
our trembling fruit creation—
we push ourselves away—go hungry.

And sometimes we don't even know
what we've made, some hearty
fresh blend of fruit and spice,
and all the summer-honeyed countryside
wafts desire through the center of our home,
and we partake of what's taken years
to insufflate with love, our little golden dome,
yeasty with hope, salty with sorrow,
tender after all our hard work,
something hot, delicious, and satisfying.

Carpentry

Stuck, on a warped, old track,
our shoji screens, that came with the house,
just won't budge beyond the bulge
in our living room floor, anymore,
to let in the garden's full delights.
But we love the screens, their intricate
winding scrollwork so lovely in light.
And thus we watch how the carpenter
lays on his hands to think through
the old wood, to free it
for our new history, tapping here
and there, listening with knowing fingers.
"Don't give me painkillers!"
he says. "I tell the doc I got
to know what's wrong." He casts
his air bubble adrift in his level
with some unseen projecting apparatus,
older than the wood, and our logic aside,
so that across his fingers the future slides
its gliding shoji screen shadows,
as he changes the hardware, shaves nine doors
to fit each kink in track that won't
lie flat, so each uniquely sized
screen slides somehow smoothly home.

So I am going to my level with breath,
and building my mental screen. I hear
the humming white noise of wholeness
in my hall of radiance, where conflict
cannot come, though ingrained insecurity
warps what's first projected as I track
my husband with his arm around another,
and her arm is around him, sparking
my jealousy synapse, and they pull apart,
the way they did, that day. Then gently,
I slide the screen to the right, the past,
and slide in the future screen from the left.
In the calm bubble of self-composure,
the loveknot is my husband and I, as we
entwine in talk and touch, in resplendent woods,
where I know his smell, taste his sweat.
When I open my eyes and enter our living
room, he smiles above his book
he shuts, and there, before our open
shoji screens, the whole garden
entering us, we come sliding home.

For Lillian

Because she loved beautiful things—
life's wish to recur in the palindrome
of amber beads on a string from her mother
I wear now with her soft-clasp earrings—
we sauntered through death's exquisite necklace
along the shoreline wreathed with the living
seaweeds and shelled secrets we shared,
each bending for a delicate beauty to show
the other, what pearly shadings, what
haunting, yearning voices to press
to our inner ears, to love. We laughed
at the many-chambered anecdotes of my son,
her grandson, that sea urchin revealing
the many-chambered anecdotes of her son,
my husband. At first timidly sandpiping
and rapidly retreating from our crashing currents,
we ventured further, two women, arm in arm.
We got knee-deep in tidelore, scooping
from the bottom, stuffing our pockets past reason
as we spoke, leaving how to string all these
little shelters for the art of later
recollection—"That's a second! Toss it!"
she'd say, her eye for beauty
honed from long, lonely strolls
along the Floridian sands, where
her husband, a lifetime away upstairs
in his papers and alcoves of anger, insisted
they move in his retirement—"A keeper!"—

I see her skirted suit ballooning
in air, her back humped with life,
and how bright the wind and spume became
in the continually coiling light as we turned
our talk this way and that, taking
armfuls of these senseless beauties upstairs,
where the refrigerator that was never big enough
was magnetically metamorphosed to an art gallery
with our faces and our journeys she could wander
when we flew back home to New York,
our luggage more full than when we'd arrived
from her stashing brownies and the gifts she shelled
out her whole allowance dole upon,
with her private womanly advice—
"Never get caught like me without
your own account!"—and her week's "firsts"
in cowries, sundials, limpets, lucines,
olives, oysters, welks, turkey wings.
She lamented I didn't wear jewelry
and said someday I'd change my mind.
Her light out, the art gallery is closed,
so I'm stringing treasures from her shoreline
because she loved beautiful things—

Sustenance

At night, when slugs come out
from cracks in our driveway, and push
their hungry, pasty beings
up the doorway ledges, along the window glass,

when cratered snails lose their way
up the sterile lampposts, that are lit
for some other kind's vision,
feebly feelering the vastly black universe,

this unhoused self of darkness,
that would dip like a deliberate hummingbird beak
down deep dream-sweet feed funnels,
on iridescent, metaphysically winging words,

this lame, night-debris feeder, that knows
the crawl and the crush of slugs and snails
beneath larger feet in our garden,
this heart, on its own muscle, pushes out again.

The Biology Lesson

Dissection day in the lab,
he would bleed light to us
under cold fluorescents,
after formaldehyded frogs
—the stench of beast.

This frog, engulfed by his knuckles,
was alive!

And we were summoned to watch
the insignificance of its pea-green flesh,
squirming,
as he stretched it out on a block of wood.

It was alive
as he plunged in a pin
through the left little leg—
its well-shaped muscles immobilized.

It was alive
as he pierced through the right
with its two little scars.

The point of the lesson—
the course of blood—
so no anesthesia. *It would
stop the heart*, he said.

One arm got free and reached
into air, waving,
pushing against his omnipotent thumb.

An inexplicable smile spread across his face
before he stabbed the pin
through that freed little hand.

The last limb was easiest—
the pin slid right in.

Pinned alive, so we might receive it,
a frog, O God, it was just a frog—
I wanted to run—
but the lesson wasn't over.

It was alive
as he sliced open the arm
that had waved,
peeled back the thin skin,
pinned it open.

A stain spread over
the block. Flowing
down the sides of the wood,
its life began
leaking away
as sand in an hourglass.

Hurry up and look! he admonished
and set the scope on a beating vessel,
so we might bear witness—
and there it was—his smile
again, a flickering lesson
in his little head spears.

Then he worked with his blade,
cracked open its small,
heaving chest, and revealed
its naked, pulsating heart—

akin to our sanctuary,
whose distant throbbing he
could not hear beneath the blade
of his Caesarean delivery into death
in the stink of cold knowledge.

My turn, told to look in,
I thought of Hawthorne's Dr. Chillingworth,
the probing violation
of a living heart—
and wanted to run—but the lesson
wasn't over—and I looked in—
because he told me to.

It was a lesson of flesh
and tissue and tears, taking
thirty years, but it's
not over yet—to see—

To see all the delicate, fragile
layers of life that could be pierced,
punctured, peeled back, and probed,
who could count the creative ways,
with acid or rope or electric prods,
unscrambling DNA and high-tech bugs
for all the ferocity of bioterrorism,
skin scorched, bones broken, hearts exposed,
the black shadow dangling
from the tree of life.

And I have wondered down the toll
of years since my first compliance—
How else? How else?

One Small Kindness

Each day my neighbor
carries his dog
all the way to the park
because she's too old
to walk so far
while her puppy frisks along
high spirited beside them.
Motionless with arthritic ice,
her little Yorkshire legs
know surrender and hope
cradled together
in his peaceful arms
that don't make the news
as he carries the blur
of hours into deep dark
with what matters.

Sheltering Cats

Hail like thorns falling everywhere from nowhere
but within a row of garbage cans—dubbed *Cat Condos*—
we laid on their sides, lined with old carpeting,
sweaters, and other remnants of our molting lives
that make warmth a growing need in a windy world.

Through closed lids, we opened thresholds,
so their windows are doorways, as seeing is entrance
and a means of leaving our own little places,
so into that part of their lives, clearly theirs,
we can feed on such sweet, furry faces!

To each a name, our eyes widening from each identity,
like Uncle Brownie, who nurtured his sister's litter,
and Swirl, too antsy to eat with the crowd,
Renalda and Hot Pants, a pair loyal for years,
so they're the ones sheltering our loving alchemy.

Cat Funeral

Between the warmth of their furry circle
and the sting of another late spring,
between the cankered clouds we fly with
through the window and the muddy leaf litter,
across our patio, Dilly, grand matriarch
of generations who live in our backyard,
emerged from her black, 3-foot lean-to
with it in her mouth, a dangling smidgen
of senselessness. She dropped it at their feet—
the ones we call Blizzard, Snowy, and Swirl
she'd faithfully nursed in that lean-to
all through last winter's blitzkrieg snow,
Silly-Dilly and Dilly-Dally we'd named for her,
Chocolate, Brownie, Stubby too—all of them grown
and benignly ignored by her, except for
an occasional head-bumping—translation: "Hi,
how ya doin!"—just passing in our garden.

And between this morning's op-ed debate
on whether Spanglish is a proper language
and Nike's women workers brutally run
to light-headed enlightenment and collapse
in Vietnam on International Women's Day,
between Aunt Helen's cold phone lines
"Don't be a wussy!" to Mike to cope
with his mother's sudden death from stroke,
I watched, behind the glass, somewhere between
a distant bystander of another bruised world
and the "catwoman" the neighbors call me.
Somewhere flesh and fur interface and know.

Each grown cat sniffed and pawed the dead one.
Then Dilly picked it up, and they followed,
a slipshod litter procession, across
the patio, and down the garden steps,
along the lawn to the thrashing hemlocks' bed.
She clawed a hole, and they hovered around
as she buried her baby, and none made a sound.
Who could say for sure what was going on
out there in the throes of our backyard,
but her task done, she returned to our patio,
her familial retinue following behind…

And they wrapped themselves around
her, enfolding her, and licking her,
enfurring her with all they were,
upgathering her hair, her ears, her eyes,
moistening her translationless all over,
in sympathy's universally mothering tongues.

Central Park

Shooting uphill, through the slow-climbing crowd,
the weight of his whole body balanced on his blade
of wheels, the skater vies for flying time
with disks, rings, boomerangs, and winged things,
footballs with fins, and frisbees sent sailing
hundreds of feet at a toss, as people are filling
the skies with aerobatic stunts, and scribblers try
with paint or pen on the grass to surf on
that same airflow at the leading edge,
to create their center of lift with image or language.
Into that charmed current go the speeding
bikers and skaters, helmeted like pilots,
with trailing vapors of joggers, high
on their hormones, a flock of funky crow puppets
in purple jackets and sunglasses, rocking and rapping
in sync, with hugs for the clapping, tapping kids.
New York's native kaleidoscope is climbing the notes
in caftans and jeans, saris and jumpsuits—
a ring of steel drummers is inviting guests
to sit in and take off, a guy plays light
on a homemade stringed gourd etched with a star,
a venerable jazz combo is pitching
over old songs, raising a sing-along,
as couples start rotating in tango flight
or flights of embrace out on Great Lawn,
where a lakeside crooner is grabbing the sun
on the mike as it leaps from guitar strings.
radio dials, pen clips, and flying rings,
in iridescent, overlapping scales aloft,

risen from the green grass sea of humanity
stretching summer's soaring, gliding, defying gravity
with a volleyball or kiss, a pressing lip
at a concave edge to a disk, brush, wind
instrument or word, at the megaphone of a film maker,
who looks just like Woody Allen, jump-
cutting to a horse and buggy ride, as girls
are gaining altitude through a turning rope,
each starting from a separate jumping-off place,
where fear is known to jump in the throat,
and some think of the junkies and muggers high-tailing
from dark corners for whatever they can lift,
or feel the more frightening grasp of mugger within,
and into that charmed current warmed by air
defying the hidden labor of lift from place,
NYers keep whisking me right off my page.

"Gableshu"

Only minutes left, and yet
students lift their heads from a test
to say "Bless you!" to a sneezer.
Drifting at my desk, I wonder

why there is no "Bless you!" for coughs,
or coitus, flatulence, or mouthing off,
when each, like a sneeze, is a spraying out,
through which, it was believed, your soul left

your body to fend on its own unholiness.
Did they think the soul left only through the nose?
Then what's the upshot of having two nostrils?
That could lead to divided souls,

lots of expelled, divided souls,
free-floating, unblessed, in the universe alone.
I hate to think some poor sneezer
or wheezer was left a soulless geezer

because I was the sole unblessing bystander,
distracted in my garden from my tie to this passerby
during rose, cold, or hay fever,
flu, spore, smog, or whatever

season for sneezing. Yet I must confess,
as a teen atheist, I took an oath of non-blessing,
seeing the quick-fix, knee-jerk comment
at a reflexive sneeze as no skin

off the blesser's nose, while the charlatan
in sheepskin blessing of good Samaritan
often slied away at the slightest personal jeopardy,
so a cheap "Bless you!" was just hypocrisy.

Loafing at ease, I invited my sneeze
by looking up at the sun to release
a little tickle in my nose this morning,
and hoped the approaching stranger said nothing,

made no requests for divine favor
to reinvite my soul, that I conceive
in a sieve universe, shaky still. Silently,
he waited till he could look directly

at me—and then he said, "Gableshu!"
I almost said, "Thank you." I knew
the routine. But then I saw into his eyes—
so I blessed him too. Why wait for a sneeze?

Lakeside Sinfonietta

The Adirondacks

Between the mountain-shawled lake and the seated,
shawled adults, between the shelled musicians and rows
and rows of chairs, like something out of a good dream,
        children come skipping…

Over the lakeside boulder, out onto the grass,
before stacked programs and bound committee schedules,
carrying the winds' and reeds' idioms in their beings,
        children come cartwheeling…

Along ardor's overflowing edge, on wet,
muddy, who-cares soles, loose in their limbs
and fiddling with Mozart with their whole bodies,
        children come caroming…

Upgathering spin-drift and sparkle, on airs of extension,
with all the glimmer of 1000 lakes and desires
they know in their blood, as Debussy is made flesh,
        children come twirling…

As one flings up grass and marrows through an explosion
of runs, another falls into laughter and violins'
sweet staircase of strings, as all sonority is stepping when
        children come lofting…

Beyond whatever whittles through the woodwinds of human purpose,
beyond the ruining tempo, the mortality in our stars,
with wondrously squandering energy, on pivots of identity,
        children come prancing…

Funneling Sun

Sometimes I play a game with myself
that my wish to go back in time
to this very day and this
very bounty of my life
at this very moment has been
granted from some high-walled
future I can't begin to imagine
and I am younger as I am
but hadn't seen over those high
concrete blocks in everyday living
to bask in the luminous lake
the sunshine makes as it touches
and spreads through my mind
the abundant crop of tomatoes
beefing in pots on the patio
where licking their fur to shiny
three cats leisurely curl
as Mike licks his finger and parts
sunlight in the province of his book
and bids me enter the expedition
of undaunted courage with him
in our backyard with Meriwether Lewis
and ringing enters the native sunshine
signaling from those we love
calling from the interior
of their own private expeditions
maybe our son and his wife reporting
on the bid they made for a house
maybe my mom bidding me
to drive her to see dad in the home

or a friend organizing the Friday brunch
to feast together after Thanksgiving
with all our children and all their loves
and I am so happy in this wellspring
my wish has come true to my life

In the Hospital There Are Moments

When Tara, my Hindu roommate, stricken
speechless and paralyzed by stroke,
streams into tears as I lift
her fallen gown back onto her shoulder
and she leans forward for a hug,

when I say "Good night, Roomy"
to the black woman with MS who's been
in and out of this ward since 1987
and she pulls open the curtain between us
and moonlight streams onto my bed,

when the Polish woman on the gurney
on her way to surgery at 5 a.m.
grasps my hand I've wriggled my way
to the edge of my bed to offer
with a stream of wishes for luck and time,

there are moments I know my self
and the totality of the universe are no different,
moments my mind is in every cell of my body.

From *Inside the Embrace*

Here in the Wind

I forgive you, God, for not existing.
It was really more difficult to forgive my mother,
who did exist, for her absence of kindness
to her husband, who defended her right to insult him,
and to her children, who weren't yet mothers, didn't yet get
to see their mother's absence of mother
in their own childhood, nor in their mother's childhood,
when she kept seeing her father pinching women
in subways that rattled through her senses
on lifelong, subterranean, one-way tracks,
that never brought her father back to her mother,
to bring her mother back to her, nor she to us—absence existing,
like you, God—that's how strong need is.

Remember how I kept confiding in you when I was 8,
like confiding in my mother, who didn't listen either
with her ear pressed to her mother's grave—"Mama!
"Mama!... Mama!... Mama!..." Such a long line of need—
maybe it goes all the way back to Eve.
I don't need her to hear me now though, now that I know
solitude has the most attentive ears.
And I forgive you, God. And I forgive her.
It was really more difficult to forgive myself,
because I couldn't save her from herself,
when she leaped to her mother through the open window—
and survived from the fall of her stories, to be my broken child.

Unlike my broken doll, I couldn't tie her pieces together
in my childhood, when I was told to keep my eye on her,
and she felt divided by my arms yoked to friends, as we'd go
singing unseasoned songs through streets of our mutual yearnings,
so she invented stories of their betrayals, their parties
without me, as she boxed out the warm comforts of neighborhood,
and boxed up our clothes to move us far away,
but not far enough away to find herself threatened again—
"You love your father more! Admit it!"
My double kisses to reassure her like pasty SWAK seals
on letters left unopened, her fears hovering, as staticky shadows
in the face of love there, beneath her inattentiveness to the man
who carried the weight of her handbag, her groceries, her insults,
her lust for praise, her denied need for him into their old age—

when whether a child loves the needier or more giving parent
becomes irrelevant recognizing a deeper connection among them all.
And God, who does not exist, that's how I came to understand
spirituality, believing in weekly groceries I hauled to their home,
overwhelming my mind beyond its simple sorting out
of their pills and deeds in little labeled cubicles, riding the sirens
with them into emergency room after sorrowful emergency room,
watching her rise in his Parkinson's weakness to care for him,
upwelling her strength, every day, for two years, in their home,
as she cared for him in a hospital bed, upwelling love's prophecy
with each of our lives becoming larger than any of our limitations.

And even more than the driver who ran over Snowy, our cat,
more than the surgeon who took my inner ear and left me
with meningitis, the vandal who trashed my rock garden,
more than the anonymous student who posted I shouldn't
be allowed to teach, and more than a dear friend's power
to silence my giggling over a young ice-cream scooper's
"You're the prettiest gal I ever saw!" with "That guy's retarded!"
more than my wondering was this insidious hurt, inside
just another party without me my mother taught me to invent,
or just another betrayal of my own lust for praise—
through all the wind-breaking reflections in the window glass—
it was really more difficult to forgive myself
for being the driver in the crash that cracked my mother's ribs
on our way to her doctor, put her on a respirator for months,
a pipeline to her throat rendering her speechless, as her eyes
faithfully followed photos I showed her of her great-grandchild
she would never get to hold to the voice of her body,
my sister and I holding her hands, unable to accompany her
while I sang the lullaby she used to sing to me,
and the doctor disconnected her from all the machinery
that couldn't save her, any more than we.
It's all been one long exercise in forgiveness.
And I forgive you, God. And I have come to forgive me.

And oh so many little peeves a child can color, string-up like
beads, wear as costume choker around the throat, self-decorating,
as time flakes off particular edges and memory smoothes.
But these genuine salt water pearls she gave me
I wear, not for pained beauty, but for the sheer luster
of her hearty laughter telling a dirty joke, her radiantly
crying "I'm peeing! I'm peeing in my pants!"
for the luster of the delicate eggs we peeked at together inside
a sparrow's nest, beneath our bucket on our fire escape,
for the dazzling sheen on her hair when she entered the sunshine,
smiling, chirping from a bookkeeping job, where she was happier,
and we'd waited in the car with dad to take her back home,
for the opalescence of her off-key, high-pitched notes, notes she
couldn't quite reach to songs, whose resounding words failed her,
yet she kept singing as she stirred the bubbling crock pot
of red and green peppers, yellow squash, and mushrooms,
of purple onions, peas, and eggplant, and called it Spanish rice,
as she rocked me through ear abscesses, colds, and flu,
teased out luster on my hair, plucking out nits, strand by strand.
Teardrops of forgiveness are more like these pearls I wear,
each a globe of wholeness, each irritating grain contained,
unabraded, built upon, like strong memories made ever-lasting
in forceful emotions, layer upon layer, grown to give off
lustrous multihues when looked at in an all-encompassing light.

Cleft Palate

The hole in the roof of my mouth
is haunted
by the ghost of my breath.
It resurrects a nasal wildness
through the soft fleshy home
where my words live.
It frightened my mother
when I was a child—it
made milk run through my nose,
sucked spaghetti like smoke up a flue
through my head, and made me sneeze.
She was ashamed
I spoke unlike other children
whose voices flowed as crisp spring air,
while mine nosed around,
drowning in air,
or nose-dived in the aping airs
of an insecure kid's pinched-nose mock.
She bought me M&M's for sweetness,
her hand in mine, the best part,
and took me by subway to Mount Sinai
speech school, where elocutionists tried
to exorcise it by exercise,
my blowing at a ping-pong ball
across a white sheet of paper
as if I were executing my words.
And that, I suppose, is how initially
I felt my cleft palate as a spirit
haunting a collection
of calamities and pleasures.

Silently and Ceaselessly

They're on their honeymoon now,
        on the shoreline of a lake's early spring,
gently rippling as a dream that inspires
        such ruddiness in their cheeks, a rosy solace
                in their outlooks as they look off
                        past the frame of their rowboat
in which their legs so intertwine,
it's as if they've only three between them,
        and they're so young, young enough to be my children,
            as they sit at the prow, balanced on mere promise,
        listening to the songs of this lake
            that are for their ears only,
        as silently and ceaselessly these songs
would come to nourish the seeds their bodies believed in,
        and they hold each other around their necks,
            their heads touching, their hair intertwined,
so thick, dark, and raised with waves,
        redolent of the rippling that would carry them
to the distant side of the lake,
despite the efforts of their oars,
        disarmed by trust and sickness,
by anger, loneliness, and fear,
        but mostly, they would be disarmed by love,
            a gently, rippling, limitless discovery,
        and here where more than one thin nail
            keeps them from the gravity of time,
                beyond the wormhole-eaten corner
      they can't see through,
            as Big Bros. carts off their crystal bowls,
        they're on their honeymoon now.
Hilda and Ruby Leibowitz   Lakewood, New Jersey—1941

Morning

It comes like a call from someone in the past,
some old friend we'd forgotten on a swing
in memory, sweeping us into those striations
of rose and gold, hints of purple pulling us
through some sorrowful vortex, as she pumps,
and we begin to stir up those subtler hues,
little vibrancies we'd learned from her,
and from so many others we've met along the way,
as we are so much more than our given primaries,
as our people palette can save us our lives,
and just as our small eyes can contain
that vastness of sky, I tell you, it's that beautiful,
this little shift in perspective, to forgive.

Here

Here,
in the wind,
out of the ooze of evolution,
the most immaculate conception
is love.

Piano Lessons

His were scales, bells that jingle, Billy Joel,
and then the leafing-out of his fingers to light
blossoming mellifluence
from deep within those subsonic boy bones,
rooted in private, tympanic canals.

Mine were off the keyboard,
cheering at Mrs. Fabricant's recitals,
taking note after note of my own
imperfect, corrective gaze
at the boy who was all elusive tones
aching to sound their barest, breathing colors.

My onplaying dilemma stemmed from this—
though I could never play his piano,
that old baton was put in my hand,
and I so wanted to drop its deadweight drag,
for who doesn't know too many nos,
and how they spoil that littleboysong.

With each pointed pencil's poke at his fingers,
with each of Mrs. Fabricant's "Up like soldiers!" spike,
I flinched for him, and for all his music lessons ahead
that would penetrate through a sharpness to his skin.

Now mine is in scraping the scale from the wood,
extracting the "Twinkle Twinkle…" sheets from within
the bench, maintaining a soldier face for the movers
clocking in, as they carry this off like some
grand sonorous spirit of my son inside the wood,
with the Hardman just some superficial label
on a body all scars and scratches,
each a little resounding piano man
leaving again and staying forever.

Maxine's Mandolin

When the terrorists struck the Pentagon
she took out her mandolin—
and as his desk was swabbed for anthrax
she stroked her mandolin again—
her inaudible music in earthy scents
sent airborne notes of crinkle-cut carrots
wafting to him on healing waves
of wild marjoram wands—
just touchings of celery strings—
as she played a red potato plectrum—
moving her wrist rapidly
back and forth for her tremolo
measures in waffle-worked disks—
and as he was being evacuated
down disaster's ever-lengthening hallway—
she tuned the peg with a slight twist
to her delicate parsnip pitch—
and sent its pinwheels beating out
her promises through the calamities in the wind—
to lure him from harm with an ancient faith
in her biochemical lovesong—

Aviva's First Belly Laugh

As Aviva bobbles and bounces, empowered
        upon her daddy's chest, the bjorn holds her upright
                beneath the swaying trees, so she's high, so high—

where the buzzing bits of being zip through air,
        where she must feel some newgrown wholeness
                toward the world she faces with freed arms and legs,

as daddy's strong body moves as her own.
        She babbles with bubbles, her nostrils go Gothic
                with effort to say her meaning, her meaning unseen

yet catching in bits of air bursting in rainbow film.
        There's a carpe diem cry the sky makes sometimes,
                for no special reason, none other than here, here,

in its own airiness, as when a family
        goes out together for a walk, to no
                special place, just down the block

and winding through the neighborhood park.
        So I swing my granddaughter's hand with mine,
                skip large, more up and down than ahead,

so she might feel she's on her own legs,
        and I sing about skipping to some Loo,
                some strangely familiar place of sheer air

rising as joy's kindling is igniting.
        First times are always mysterious,
                as waking from a wooden, wintry place

where buds are pushing their purple, pulsing urgencies
    through the yielding, cold spring—That's her smile
        cracking open, into the first time she laughs out loud

and long, at what? from someplace deep where
    she has swallowed a galloping pony, giddy-
        giddy weee, giddy-giddy weee. What could

be funny to a mind without a leg
        to stand on irony's discrepant ground?
                Giddy-giddy weee, giddy-giddy we

too get giddy-giddy, and wonder what clicked
    from black and white to color for her, like oranges
        just popping up from nowhere, giddy-giddy as

when TV's "Show of Shows" first went rainbow in our
    living rooms, we too giddy-giddy, in the spaces between
        all languages, on this hearty energy of being, we too

go tumbling from within, releasing our bellies
    like inhabited lakes, we too go giddy-giddy,
        go giddy-giddy weee, go giddy-giddy weee—

Backpack Girl

May she linger like this, unhurried
        by have-tos, as she sits and stirs
                her song into swimming colors

shocked with shells, and leaves laced
        with sand, and floating bits of seaweed,
                as she ladles her bucket by the sea with foam

from waves, and myriads of miniscule
        living ingredients, like little motors
                with which a little girl generates

such apple-pizza goodness—"Taste!"
        We all want what she scoops out
                upon a sieve for each of us,

dripping them nameless and unseen
        into gobbling sand beneath our feet,
                as leaving-time reminds it's time

she pulls with each strap onto each shoulder,
        as she gladly rushes into the feel of the clasp
                of her already agenda-seeking backpack.

Cleomes

It's not about the flowers
but who we are   as we tend
    to their spidery pinkish wisps
        to seed-pouched splendor

    It's because we bend
before them   with meal offerings
    as   we   wonder   if
        beauty   like   God

    didn't   really   exist
would we   will-o'-the-wisp
    petal by petal   by   petal
        have   to   invent

    with   our   fists   full
of white powdered   animal bones
    as we   stoke   what we know
        of earthen fireworks

    so as they release their
small starbursts   they feed us
    on   air-   loomed
        essences … … …

It Is In the Interruptions

Making love on paper sheets,
writing my way home,
just doesn't cut it—
I brake for life—
leave my metaphors idling—
lift the receiver off the hook,
engage my voice to a resistant ear,
"You have to reopen our eaves
and let it out!" I plead again
with the leaders-and-gutters guy.
The squirrel we'd thought moved out
was pacing and scraping all night.
It kept scratching its frantic
little life into our dreams overhead.
Too often I lose the important hasp
paging image to image.
It is in my clasp on this one life
as I raise my voice to save it.
"Please, you have to do it now!"
Despite his hectic day, his cutting laugh,
he comes, opens it more than he knows,
a doorway for weaving its nestlings'
furry stand into our papers and plans.

I abandon a participle almost a corpse,
hanging it mid-mind and kicking,
to lift the latch on the room-sized cage,
release Star, my niece's "Hello! Hello!"-whipping,
wing-walloping, crest-flaring, raucous
white wave of a nuzzling Cockatoo—

It enters my alien human space.
It tilts its head, relishes my back rub.
I flap my arms, it flaps its wings.
It squawks, I squawk.
We bob our necks in sync.
"I think I'm engaged!" I tell my husband,
as we sit on the sofa with it between us,
munching its almonds, waiting for Jenny to heal.

In fur and feathers, flesh and flanks,
it matters more even in steam,
as it is rising now, so savory
with scents of rosemary, ginger, and thyme
from the soup I stir for my neighbor
sick from chemo and fear in this one life
that struggles so to stand its ground.
I have her key. I get it.
I let myself in.

Scraps at the Zoo

"Stop that crying
or I'm gonna give you good!"
The fleshy woman yanked
the seed of her pain
into the bathroom stall,
shut the door with a smack.

"Why didn't you go
when I took you! Now you'll wait
till I'm good and ready!"
She cast his sentence
without a word
from the arm-casted boy.

Later, in the netted
house, he tore tissue wings
from butterflies in his
scrappy fingers,
felt their fluttering
moment going limp.

Heads Up and Out of Sight

Even loneliness can pass through cells,
get projected onto the chatterful air,
join the grand autumnal chirring through the trees,
back to school, drifting up to the sky—high
stats of the Mets, and who dumped who
at Bogart's Bar, who won't be home to see
aunt Martha, and why "It" "is the weirdest
thing!" "can't ever last!" "just didn't
come out right!" "will all get done!"
as she crosses the quad, tense but in the beat
of interclass footsteps entering the satellite service area,
so walking is no longer companionless,
cold stinging through her au courant ripped jeans,
amid all those loud, purposeful voices
not talking to the person next to them,
and the more they press their ear cells,
the less they hear who's right there,
as she ritually speed dials no one
to speak aloud to someone.

Semester's End
  (For Eng 002—11)

There's a long, lonely foreverness
while I am looking at these young faces
through a familiarity that has swelled with time
into a kind of ripening binding,
and knowing it's the last time,
with all its incompletions,
inexorable opportunities missed, muffed, ignored.

Better not to know, for I begin to think
of all the words I could never write
and never will to them—
to Kim, too shy to speak above raw whispers,
to Pete, whose thoughts repel each other on the page
but could articulate aloud how misplaced
"the fountain from … which [Othello's] current runs,"
to Josh, whose best friend was shot down in the street.

And of all that I did scrawl across their margins,
across their headings, upside down behind
the substance of their labored strivings—
with swollen eyes, he confesses to me,
"I never got to sleep to do this one, Mrs. T!"—
I do believe there is a thesis in all this—
so I keep working—and the tense shifts this semester

Into next semester, entangling time with faces
throughout my heart like some vast, sprawling vine.
If there is a coherence behind the pushing, prodding, asking
for elaboration, evidence, example, personal voice,
so that we see what we clearly can't see,
so that we feel what we passionately ignore,
as together each one of us leaves—

Perhaps someday, when this binding thins
and cracks open somewhere we cannot foresee,
inexplicably, some human blossoming—

Jasmine

If I had to name it as fragrance,
I'd say it's that full-body spray, in winter,
after a long and achy jog,
its unexpected reachings
reminding me of my mother's Miguet,
or her White Shoulders in my hair,
her perfumed bath soap sudsing,
giving off visible breaths of peace,
from farther than memory's headwaters,
through her long fingers, and I am
strangely refreshed on this coldest morning,
in this inhaled stillness.

And it's that ambling's sudden aroma, in spring,
from way down tangly, vined lanes with Mike,
where our Charleston's sweet, lush loving
is slipping, as an ambrosial fragrance
knows how to slip, unscathed and delicious,
through all those little, hurting thorns, along the road.

Along my heart's wild passageways,
there's a purely insinuating, sourceless scent,
I call it jasmine because it keeps learning another
way, another way, to catch me wholly
by surprise, and it's been meandering here a long time,
this richly exquisite, forgiveness tracery.

From *Hidden in Plainview*

Night Vision

Late at night, I look out my window, across
the darkness separating me from my closest neighbor,
my friend some thirty years, dying of cancer,
on hospice in her own home, her light still on—
an all-night vigil across that long way
brings me nearer to her as she travels farther
away, like a distant star, more visible than my own garden,
in the great darkness that surrounds our lives,
our planet, the small globes of our seeing.
Friendship is that gleam of light
made brighter at night, when everything changes scale.
She never will enter my home again,
nor call from the edge of spring, all excited—
"Home Depot's got mandevillas in for a song!"
How we'd scale the various nurseries in town
for just the right height and shades of dahlias,
and showed each other our blooms come to light,
our children and grandchildren, her paintings, my poems,
and bought good-luck herons for each other's flower beds,
she called hers Gayl, I called mine Flo.
I can't access her shortcuts, one town to another,
nor find that exotic nursery our serendipitous meanderings
brought us to, and then the crying, side by side
at some gloomy movie, in memory's theater,
that backward crush to singularity
each relationship is.
I can barely see the floor beneath my feet,
yet far better than in broad daylight,
I can see the unfathomable distance that contains us,
and binds her dying to my living heart
like some special song of rebirth.

Three Weavers

Someone has threaded a wee basket
securely through the branches of a tree,
and it has made all the difference
to the bird whose nest has fallen,
to that generous hand who held his own
quivering happiness as the bird's beating breast,
and to me weaving my afternoon's way
into that resonating vicinity
of secret little gift.

Our Daily Bread

How could anyone smell the fresh
baking bread rising in the air
and not want to live?

Next door, the bird lover's morning hair
looks as if it's come through
night's private, turbulent wind

as she opens challah rolls, strews
rye too, from her well-husbanded pantry,
onto the street, lingers in her thick widow gown.

Onto the cement shoreline, hurry-scurry
gulls and sparrows indulge. Then one swoops
down from where clattering cans sound like geese

clamoring inside double trash bags looped
to her bike, as wind spreads the wings
of her billowing rain slicker she wears

even on this hot, sunny day. Reaching
into the modest abundance, she scoops, pockets
from the common language of bread, and cranks ahead.

Sight Behind Sight

Sipping coffee at my kitchen table,
      I meander along the streams of the county
         of my birth, the Bronx blooms

are reopening in the Botanical Gardens,
      as silence amplifies my view, I climb,
         as then, the craggy ways to my secret solace

atop a rocky outcropping, my girlhood's
      500-year-old gneiss and schist spot,
         a boulder I hold within my being—

I overlook the sharp-needled blue China fir,
      and see again its majesty within my pavilion,
         the rose garden's rainbowed resplendence,

the Iranian tree trunk's black and white
unconscious precision, the broad blue
      Atlas cedar's spreading self-possession

like long dense sentences
      punctuated by trilling birdsong.
         Like that deciduous dawn-redwood,

I too have dropped some part of myself
      in wintery cold, but I too remember
         like a living fossil knows how to survive.

The mica-flecked, jagged boulders
      have drawn me since I was a child.
         I have known the hard ledges

like memories defied by new-green
growing softness. Some poised power
        of Bronx rock resides within my solitude.

And in conversation with my zumba buddy
        from Jamaica, or my rose-master neighbor
                from Korea, sharing his wisdom with me

on light and blight, with my dear friend Fyina
        from Russia, rearing her psychologist child,
                the woman I met yesterday who walked me

into her Puerto Rican unsnowing homeland,
        unspoken energy ripples from each one's
                private outcroppings, from whatever spot

one chooses, to sit in tranquility,
        where sooner or later some beauty appears,
                abounds and surrounds and permeates us all.

The Mah Jongg Players

Upon the vast gymnasium floor
polished into a glossy pool
of light, clasped by late autumn's
great waning days grown shorter,

and shorter, these four women are
the only ones left at the senior center,
after the lunch crowd, the card players,
the loners, even the chitchatterers

have gone onto that brittle crunch
of leaves, scattering for home. They
pull their chairs in much closer
around anticipation's delicious center

that gathers them around a bridge table,
where they bridge their lone-ridged lives
with ivory flower tiles clattering a familiar
welcome. They keep learning, "keep sharp!"

they brag, with this year's new patterns
of bams and cracks, as others show up on their
aging faces, but these they're determined
to master, on racks they can lift with bare,

cracked hands, stack their small riches upon,
defy the greater stacked deck whispered
by wind before the long weeks of deep snow.
Sometimes they bicker over their moves,

like moves they might have made in the larger game.
Yet here within their wee community,
once a week, edgy as they are
to win something much vaguer

than the few dollars they wager,
edgy as they are about leaving too late
into dark, or too soon into husbandless rooms,
already anticipating next week's game,

as each contains her own unspoken, broken
ivory towers, they keep rebuilding their ivory
walls with grandchild tidbits, and laughter bursting
between them, to free them from redoing old requiems,

these four mah-jongg playing, Plainview women,
who look like fat-bellied, focused Buddhas,
absorbing some enlightening in a glossy gymnasium,
as they pass their tiles and tales around.

At the Community Center

The senior line dancers,
mostly Korean women, delicate
and lovely, they flit

through shuffle, brush,
grapevine twists, like
butterflies winging

across the floor, their flower,
where they draw their nectar
in zigzag grace, arms dipping

and sipping sweet music juices,
and then they gather, up front,
after each song, and all of us

giggle in the very same tongue,
they, at my exaggerated strokes,
and I, just because dancing

is heaven, where we can see
all those shifting shadows
shimmy out from our bodies.

Doing the Neighborly Too-Step

Busy as we are,
there's always time to stop
in our shadowy trampings—just for a jot—
to stop for the fleeting light
in a vaguely familiar face
who's from two, three, maybe four
houses, blocks away? always time
to stop to do the neighborly too-step
that follows on the "Fine!" heels
of a "Hi, how are you?" greeting
without a pause, timing is all!
"It's too hot!" "It's too raw!"
"It's too dreary!" "Too dry!" "Too humid
for my flyaway hair!" "Getting dark too early!"
"Snow's pretty but too dry for packing!"
"Sun's too weak!" "Wind's too fierce!"
"Thunder came way too close to the house!"
"It's too rainy to believe!" "Too hot for words!"
Just doing the friendly too-step,
the neighborhood glue-step,
the quick-fix weather report
for busy folks who hold hidden
those murmuring sounds from restless streams
churning in private winds too underground
to bring to light with the people they greet.
Can't imagine the sad day of news—
"Today, there will be no weather."
Whatever would we neighbors do without our "too's"
to break the ice between,
without breaking from the deeper grooves
of our own too personal moving?

Hard-Wirings

I

Along the jagged ruts and slants
in my approach to the cornered home
newly fenced, with new faces,
new belongings, purling in undersong,
spilling over and through the shiny,
spaced stakes, each so elegantly
mounted with a little hatted light,
as I jog by a few times a week,
I've seen, in piecemeal, an extended family,
an unfamiliar strangeness in
the old man's wound turban,
the old woman's draped head and body—
I've welcomed the comprehendible tongue
of the children's catch-me, catch-me frolic,
and then that tilt of the old man's head
when I dared wave into the strangeness,
to an Omar Sharif ardor in his dark, aged eyes,
a bloom of smile when I pushed off
the 911-Iraq-terrorist track,
and eased into a solace underneath
my own feet, feeling the level ground.
So smile and gesture became our idiom
leading us back to a knowing country,
and when he pointed to the sky at my wave,
I knew he was praying to a god I couldn't access,
as I knew we'd come from that same native place.

II

Does nature hunger to destroy?
Could that be why two little hats were awry?
Just that small a slant cut off their lights?
On my next jog by, the fence was fixed.
But within a week, one light was missing,
and one was hanging by its exposed wires,
while the wind's poker face brushed it back
and forth, back and forth, like my assuming mind—
wired prankster goblins or gobbling blind hate
yanked by wires to darkness like wooden heads?
On my next jog by, the fence was fixed.
But within two weeks, a stake was severed
from its ground, three hats were skewed,
and one light was smashed beyond repair.
On my next jog by, the fence was fixed.
I kept looking for the grandfather, though I knew
he couldn't tell me what hunger for darkness
struck again, and again, till torn light-veins were left—
The fence was never fixed again.
And I never saw that man again.
Just jogging by today, I kept wondering,
What strange forces decapitate our lights
and lie hidden like little curled-up dimensions,
where our invisible strings vibrate?
Peace to the man who prayed outside.
Peace to his family, his garden, his fence.

Distinctions

Not so long ago, a spider
on my kitchen wall, or a moth,
mosquito, wasp, or ordinary fly
poised on the pulling screenlight,
pushed me to go get a glass,
lift the cardboard kept in a drawer
for just such a simple rescue
of my belief I'm a Samaritan.
I domed the guest, slid
cardboard beneath at the pace
of each spindly, creeping leg.
I peered inside at cooped wings,
odd eyes seeing me as elephant tail,
a different kind of confined feelers.
I felt glad in this threshold exchange
as I stepped into its home, outdoors,
removed the barrier, watched its recovery.

Home after our vacation, carpenter ants,
countless carpenter ants were swarming
across the saddle of our doorsill.
On the sofa at night, I jumped
at their prowl-out beneath my feet—
these were big guys with toolbelts,
woodboring troops, invaders
in my home! Cannibals!
I heard they were cannibals!
I took a contract out on them.
The hit man searched behind the sofa,
showed me torn heads and limbs
of beetles they'd dragged in to eat.

What startled me most after one of them
scurried out, where I'd been sitting peacefully
in evening's loose robe, after I tissued it up,
then looked away as it struggled around,
and around, in the toilet whirlpool,
after the one or two I'd released outside,
after shouting, "You stay in your home
and I'll stay in mine!" after my night's
dream the walls were weighted
with their winged, reproducing females,
after one I'd stepped on in the kitchen,
then one I'd crushed with a fork,
after I started stomping on those in our garage,
then wider and wider outside, stomping
on those in the driveway, on those
on the sidewalk, on all those around
the trees, what startled me the most
was the ease, oh, the ease!

Of Good Fences

In the renewing season, flowers often suffice
for me to dig my way into reenchantment—
a tiny red-green dahlia prong can do it
as it pushes its life out through the earth!—
But now I must stop my groundwork
working up my spirit,
for our old fence has decayed,
and mother earth's gravity arms
are beckoning it back, as she pulls
down the boundary between us, that weight
upon our knitted-together, overlapping gardens.

What's ours, what's the new neighbors',
re-fuse in spring's lengthening and healing light.
Responsibly, we order a new fence,
neighborly, we knock on their door.
But where the fence falls, neighbors ignite—
"That fence has been way, way off, over
our property line!" they declaim.
"How can that be? We put it up.
It's been years, maybe 33! This cherry,
this holly, this crepe myrtle, we nurtured
from twigs! They're too big to move!" we counter.
"I want what is mine!"
"This underground sprinkler head
has been right here for years!"
"I want what is mine!"

We dig out old documents, surveys, and deeds.
They whip out new documents, surveys, and deeds.
We hold our bizarre diagrams up to the light,
the figures and angles as arcane as cosmic dark matter
and the deep recesses human property lines make in the mind.
"I'm getting a lawyer!" "I'll get a surveyor!"
Acid stomachs and 2 all-day surveys later,
3 stakes for $800 get planted with hammers,
and a nail is shot through the old pine tree,
to reify with authority that imaginary line between
whatever yours and ours means
for making a good-neighbors'-good fence,
that will fall through the seasons of our flesh
toward the interweaving grass above and beneath.

So we have kept our cherry, our holly, our crepe,
but they've stacked up like dead soldiers in the road,
the sawed-down arbor vitae faithfuls
we'd fed and shaped and sat with for decades.
The cypress has been yanked up by its gold threads,
and they've left a row of grey cinder blocks
to replace the yanked-up lavender and pink impatiens
I'd planted for peace on our common ground.

Though we don't know the words yet,
our lives get tuned by the wind's great song
of coming blizzards and bedazzling beauty,
and the riled dust has settled down now
from the new fence, with holes in the basketweave
interthreading our views and vibrancies—
I hear the raucous joy of their baseball game
with their boys come passing through, as I read
the Dalai Lama's *Daily Advice from the Heart,*
within the rising passionflower spirits' fragrant amplitude.

Building a Chimney

They are as in the air as song,
above the quince's sharp thorns,
high on their skeletal scaffold
with a cloudy, heavy brick pile
they   focus   into   grace
with their sun-leathered hands,
positioning   block   by   block
at   vision's   precise   edge,
and I have to tell you, because
I know you too read the papers,
that there is joy in this world,
I hear it here in my yard in
their Spanish-Italian   staccato
calls, their tidbit tales I can't
comprehend, their hearty grunts
and generous guffaws, in their
noise with tools, their boots,
the   whirring   cement   mixer,
the   motor of their worksong
being entirely something else
as they get their lines plomb,
as   they   bother   to   unearth
and   then rehouse a begonia—
"You   work   so   hard!" I say,
and he laughs, shakes my hand
in   his   sweat-soaked   shirt—
"This!   This   is   nothing!"
he   says, his testament   how
day-to-dark   work   can   be
transformed   to   transparency,
as my   flue   to   their   flute.

On Becoming a Poet

If we are but minuscule specks in a multiverse
of foaming universes bubbling forth,
where does this feeling of importance originate?
Why toil and trouble over our decisions?
Why feel what we do matters,
and why should a speck of matter feel
such density over its decisions?
But here I am weighing my specs,
far off center, in our universe of multiverses,
on a corner conglomerate of galaxies,
on some dot of a gassy Milky Way,
way out on some smaller smaller system's
mote of a planet, in some fleck of a country's
state, off on some wee wee island,
a jot of a town, down to my tiny house,
a tittle on a teeny tiny table sipping tea,
who believed her poetry professor
when he told her, "Less is more!"
and sent her off onto her page
of the multiverse of humanity to "break a foot."
See me waving through the microcosm!
Here I am, hidden in plain view.

Sundays at the Y
(For the Mid-Island Y Poets)

Twenty-three years pile Sunday reads as autumn leaves,
as we have gathered in this open, well-lit space,
each of us a private miner from darkest knowing
in some sense to be human is to be inhumane,
each of us weighted down with such hardened stuff
from long-pressurized personal living,
where our pens have been chiseling away
to get to that uniquely rare, raw precious ore,
that native self—been buried by long-denied needs.
Can't chit-chat about our ordinary intentions,
the spirit is aphasic, writes before it speaks,
but burdensome inner dramas lighten on paper,
and the sum of all points of view
is contained, somehow, in each single poem,
each poem wholly holy a magnetic needle
to steer our self-discovery by,
to a clearing ahead of heartfelt clarity,
past the spinmeister, opinion-maker clutter,
past the isolated iPod headsets.
Listening here is mostly authentic attempt,
each to each, pores to the soul opening,
a way of loving, what we came here for,
so we shake our heads and say "Aha!"
And the sum of all points of view
is contained by that one frustrated dreamer—
"Try to catch that one floating leaf!"
Eliot knew he was the last to know his own poem.
On thin pages like wings, we rise, applaud
our common needs, shown in small, cross-sectioned veins.

So we are contained in each question,
searching as a flashlight's illuminating
a wider and wider swath of humanity.
While in plain view, as autumn strips the trees
to bare bodies, a raw-powered voice
can hook us from our inattentiveness,
as if an exposed nail is snagging us by sweaterthreads,
and we become defiant to an emptiness that seems
to sculpt the substance of our beings,
as we gather here to skim our lives
like pollen off each other's poems,
the listener completing the music meant to be heard
that there is a buried miner in each one of us
who is happy to help the others out with oneself.

Why I'm a Poet

As I watch the TV tribute to Mariano Rivera,
his last time his metaphors are pitched in,
his teary farewell as he runs the bases,
and Pettitte and Jeter come to escort him
off the field where he has grown whole,
and I feel the lumpy-throated crowd,
I think of all those ballerinas
who have grown whole on their toes
and have to step down in their 30s,
and I think of that long, strange drive
taking our son off to college,
the brightness bouncing off his car ahead,
leaving him on his own unknown track,
his long look back at me saying
from then on my homers with him
would be batting underground,
he'd never need me quite the same—
and so my poem's ongoing sentence,
my teary tribute to Billy Collins, Wendell Berry,
and to all who know no mandatory cutoff
from their wholeness in fields of paper,
yet I think how we all hope to be
like those cosmic stars
that our light may survive us,
even if the game has to end.

Jellybean Lady

As he ached over a block of stone
to chisel-free his *David*, so she has ached
over jars of jellybeans to gluegun-free
her *Infantsea*, a dream wombscape, where an infant swims
and breathes, in luminous, aqua underwaters,
as viewer is made aware of the unborn's joy
moving timelessly, among vibrant angelfish,
coral and stars, crabs and algae rippling
as mind, sea, and womb are made
of what her jellybean hues give and fuse,
as viewer is made to move in close
to 7000 colored bits, painstakingly placed,
and out again, to a grandly lit, coherent
immersion, as primal voyageur
hanging at the entrance to the Y swimming pool,
as I ache now, over noun and verb,
to parse-free her pulsating tones,
from her dun security guard uniform,
and make this humble, down-tongued woman,
passersby don't connect to her *Infantsea*,
this grey, retired postal worker,
this widow of four sons, grown and flown,
I ache to make her rise, to chisel her
from her seat where she sits night
after night, at a drab desk, at the Y door,
who asks who you are, where you're headed,
but few ask her as they sign in—
if you do, she might let you glimpse
her jellybean wonders locked in her computer box,
like her replica of the Wall of Jerusalem,
hanging hidden on a wall in her home.

Electromagnetic Beauty

		Marriage
is an exchanging of
		light
particles we sometimes
		catch
sometimes miss while
		neither
can grasp exactly the
		one
in the fuzzy other in
		this
very moving flowing
		loving
that is a conversation
		ongoing
for years with no thesis no
		conclusion
all body all wave all we

On Canvases Stuck to Street

My canvases are hidden in plain view
on flattened gobs of chewing gum,
at his school bus stop, where he waited,
morning's worth yet fruity soft
and malleable in his moist mouth,
as he spat each out to climb aboard
the engines into official flags and symbols.

Thousands more gummy morning blobs
have hardened to a chronicle of his years
as he waited and played at being
the adults he thought we were.

Now, in this outbreathing of the street,
I can soften that gum without a blowtorch,
I can wake dread's tiniest hackles
to paint the trail of bloody tissues
I'd found discarded in our living room,
when I couldn't find him or the sitter anywhere,
and some maternal mechanism
sets memory's kinetic bells in motion
to summon me to that hospital again,
when his head was gashed open.

Meditating on the softening gum,
I can quick-dry spots of color
with passion's flickering lighter to the gray,
evoke his deeply felt dimensions
on the seemingly flat surface of childhood—
Voila! The shell necklace he'd saved for,
to gift with a pack of gum to the girl,
the girl's mom giving him the brush-off,
so he chewed and spat his first love's gum
there with tears, gone brittle with years.
I coat Twinkle, his cat, in white and tawny,
and with a clearer spray, I can seal in
the unconditional love that lasts a lifetime,
picture Twinkle, in his 3rd surgical bonnet,
frisking with him as he'd waited at the bus stop.

And there the shopping cart he'd peddled with,
across the largest collection of chewing gum art
he could ever imagine in the making,
his gummy gobs spreading out through my imagery
of his whimsies, his sorrows, his passions,
and this his portable tag sale,
he'd gone door-to-door, who will buy
this frog seeking some princess,
this coloring book with torn superheroes,
this school bus missing one wheel?

Yes, everything is transitory,
but this street art can't be washed away,
nor broken up for repaving, nor ruined by grime.
And I will always be his artist-in-residence,
his mom, painting beyond eyesight, in any weather.

Grandma, do you have any gum?

Six to Six

It is written slantwise to the wood grain,
bleeding through the pastel castle cut-out
frame—"Celebrating Family"—
where children get dropped off, from birth,

every 6 am, every sunny, rainy, coughing weekday,
so the yawning, young parents in overdrive can shell out
for their homes what they keenly need,
homes where at 6 pm the children reenter

in a prodigious whir of eating, bathing, off-to-bed refrains,
then moms mash toddlers their eggs for tomorrow,
pump their breasts for the freezer while e-
mailing clients, and dads sort laundered lambies, stretchies, shorts,

while phoning weekly grandchild scoops to their moms, states away,
with photo files to download online, and shouts
from the baby upstairs, a coworker's proposal to reread—
multitasking to beat the clock to bed their dream's worth

before midnight, as stretchies keep tumbling, "No way!
Not tonight!" refrains, the alarm, the bright out again,
and all down Southern Parkway and other main streets,
a cavalcade of drop-offs to Miss Sue's and Good Shepherd,

Kiddie Kollege, First Step, Child's Play,
Shalom's, Miss Kim's, Friendship Connection House,
MunchKinland, Peanut's, Just Wee Academy,
Big Chief, Creative, Lisa's Loving Care—

to each a kiss, a cubby, a loving Paige
to share (for whose own five kids pricy daycare is out,
so grandma, night-duty dad, even leaving them in the Caribbean),
and the young parents are off to their cubicled computers,

their hard-won offices of self-actualizing space
for better? for worse? feel their tugged sleeve touch
a tracery in their skin, from the clasp of the wee
fingers as he's left on his back, on a mat, underneath

a mobile, or brain-stimulating gadget for play,
till packed in a cubicled stroller for going out,
with voices unshelling as they move down the street
like a giant carton of hatching eggs in the open air,

and so each generation tries itself on its way
of being more apart to be more together,
as my mother was least together when forced to be
homebound, and we most together with her

outside as bookkeeper, her iffy quirks enough away
to endow two young girls their growing room,
and as my grandchildren cross my horizon from DC,
I link a forefinger rising from a passing giant stroller.

Water Song

Joshua and Aviva, full of laughter,
          cavorting in the freehold of their bodies,
                    in a surging power of the time of their lives,

become bobbing, black dots
          in immense ocean waves, vulnerable
                    motes, riding the music of a turning world,

as the gargantuan current
          of all that moves sweeps them
                    along into self-discovery out where

no preparation is ever made.
          Their struggle is to go out even
                    further, deeper. Mine is to keep them

afloat, closer to solid shore.
          This battle with the waves always
                    is about time. Theirs is to squander it,

to get way out and stay up on
          their own. Mine is to conserve
                    it, as time and again I have tried

to follow the dots out there:
          those of my parents, drifting
                    wordlessly away at Rockaway,

the one of my son, broncobusting
          the cold crests at Jones Beach.
                    Each bobbing dot, someone I love

out there, beckoning me, follow
        the song without measure, as we
                all rise and fall in the waves

that swallow us deep into the belly of the music.

Hungry for the Outside

Snow again, flies down with feathers
to our cat food feast beneath the eaves,
where Perky, our twentyish feral,
who just finished her matinal fare,
squeezes into her carpet-lined, garbage-can condo,
between the brick of our heated home
and the vastness of weather's waving fury.

Newcomer, Phantom Joe, a nightly streaker,
storm-stranded somewhere last night,
now bolts down barely chewed Meow Mix,
so Eric-the-Red Cardinal waits
with Buttons, his mate, atop the arbor vitae,
along with the noisy, flocking needy
grackles, blackbirds, chickadees
across our rooftop, garden fence, trees,
cheek by jowl by beak by bushy tail
of Sammy the Squirrel, who lives in our eaves.

There's a great big flitting, scurrying, weaving,
in odd congregation, lyrically around
all our mutual hungers, waiting,
all eyes on that one paper plate of provisions
we keep refilling. Never enough!

Phantom Joe's white coat dissolves
into snowy mounds as he plods away,
and the birds chirr-stir up, board down,
in the pecking order around the cat food.
Sammy waits, Eric carries food to his mate,
and we are carried out to the world
in this small hungry harmony,
fur, feathers, and flesh.

At an F.A. Meeting

Hi! I'm Gayl, and I'm a flowerholic,
I'm a plum-purple clematis popper,
it's a monkey on my back
shimmying up and down my fence spine,
I'm hooked by its grasping hooks, its

little mountain climbing gear, I'm high,
potted by every pastel pink, penta-petalled petunia
I never planted—Surprise! from last year's dropped
seeds, back again like psychedelic eye-openers—
I'm a blossom-sniffer, nectar tripper, inebriate

of anther am I and debauchee of daylily's loud
orange blare, sugar sunshine heliotrope goes
right to my head, and sweet astilbe feathers
my air till I'm flying, and I breathe deeper here
where I commune with the spirits of monkshood,

perennially faithful, it spires violet into indigo
with dark, deepset August eyes my pick-me-ups,
I am with freesia youthfulness, its flowers all
to one side as I feel inside my side-flaring ponytail
again, flushing and blushing, its colors contagious,

its fragrant amplitude shows my finite being an
opening into the vastness, and I am forever
unprepared for this happiness, forever filled
without hope for anything, flowers suffice—
"Hi, Mom!" I say to the hydrangea heads

outbreathing her ground from cuttings I took
from her globular ceruleans before selling her home,
so let celosia plumes paint my patiotown red,
as whispy cleomes cast me in their spidery spell,
set'm up heady gardenia, hollow-spurred columbine,

keep'm coming crinkle-petalled crepe myrtle,
you foxglove fingers, two-lipped dragon-mouthed snaps,
you pansy faces pushing up through the marble chips,
join me rose of Sharon with all your coarse teeth,
and you woody wayfaring lantana, most human

of all flowers to me, each dense little head
in a world of your own coloring,
I tell you, I just can't get enough,
if it flowers, I want it in my garden,
I've been to every nursery in town,

they've got my joy juice, blue angels, nose candy,
one smack swill of bougainvillea's
showy, hot sprawl, and I'm flammable,
to tie one super magenta dahlia head on
to a stake is all it takes to get me tiddly,

and every spring, in rain and mud,
I become a lush, I feel it coming on,
get my fingers soppy, sloppy, my nails
get black and broken, my skin all
cracked and scratched, I forget to eat,

my blood sugar drops, my back really aches,
and it began long ago with a screwdriver,
I got down on my knees and got my ground around
so hammered, I loosened up the hard soil,
inch by inch, until the terrain was undulating,

and what a rush when first those rosy emerald
dahlia tuber dots come smack through the earth,
I just burst open when touched by bizzy lizzy impatiens pods,
but I confess mandevilla's my favorite carouser,
its red-eyed, pink-faced frivolity from trellis clasp

dares the unsupportive air, and hangs, and hangs
until it grasps the world by the fences, and spreads
its sturdy tripping grace, erasing our boundaries
as it pushes its way into my neighbor's yard
and into the luminosity of the sky with the caw

of a blue jay the swish of the branches the scratch
of a squirrel the curl of the cat on the chair
and a palpable silence I can soak up and hear
as everywhere I go I am exactly where I am,
I tell you, I don't want to be cured—

Here's mud in your eye! Bottoms up!

Worn-Out Walking Shoes

Who would have thought when I saved them
with an unwitting toss to this garage corner,
I would come to savor them later,
with their stained tongues loosened

over maws opened wide by many ingested miles
I walked, some alone in abounding sun seeking vision,
sometimes the inventor of my own cold, curable night,
or even on the underside of joy's hush, the great rush,

or felt their scraping down sudden drops
I never saw coming. What sloughed-off skin—
dried sweat-tears salt lick—what defiant hues,
what dirty-sweet crumbs-grit—fur-blossom-bug bits—shit

got ground into the honeycomb fibers, the sole-treads,
what untraceable flecks make such a rich journey mulch?
Ground in, our grandkids' sweet ice-cream drippings
mixed with the rising beach sand, while we rolled

our bocci balls and roared with the untamed wind,
with feather barbs from the Flamingo Gardens Rescue Center,
where Mike and I hand-fed ibis and spoonbills
in the haven for the broken-beaked, the broken-winged,

and I walked among them, picking up a feel of their beings,
and from the company of each friendship, a little ship
moving me deeper into the currents of humanity,
as when I tapped my feet and shook to the peppery beat

of the Dutch folksinger in the outdoor concert
at Grand Place, on our summer vacation in Brussels,
and exchanged addresses with the jovial woman akin to me,
photographed her baby with the dark eyes like ripe cherries,

ground in, the harbored tears of the lost Korean woman
we walked with for miles, till we found her hostel,
talking all that warm dark while without the same language,
with tears soaked up from strangers weeping together,

strangers from all around the world, stunned and aching
over naked human cruelty, depicted at the Anne Frank House,
so many tears, such living testament to human compassion.
Who would have thought how everyone who's ever moved me,

from everywhere I've ever been, in these worn-out walking shoes,
would come home with me, rubbing through the skin of my life.
Who would have thought they would become like a child,
moving around inside me, enriching my being even in darkest night.

Sandy

When the raging winds downed power lines
into raw nerves, whipping about on the streets,
where we neighbors, bundled and dazed
from too-long, blue-black nights begun in afternoons,
were gladdened just to be in plain sight
of each other in the welcome mornings,
after all those Halloweenlike ogres had lurked,
ogling us in the smeared shadows of our alien rooms,
our massive trees snapped like toothpicks,
strewn as pick-up sticks across the roads,
these trees we'd considered our friends, no more,
as nature tortured and toyed with us,
smashed up homes like kindergarten blocks,
burned up some like campfire marshmallows,
flooded others like kids' water-filled balloons,
whole towns like Breezy Point reduced to rubble,
and we, the lucky ones, guilty and glad for our own roofs—
"Hey, we never knew we had a gas hot water heater!
We floated tins of cold pasta on hot water bowls!
You've got to come over. Take a hot shower!"
Mike and I played Scrabble by Yahrzeit light,
tossed out all the smelly, whiskered food,
saw our beloved Bradford pears with weapons now,
their huge arms raised right over our home, menacing,
and then they too broke down, like fragile beings from too much
stress, weakened by Hurricane Sandy, they couldn't
bear the new nor'easter's weighted snow.
And people cried openly to people they barely knew,
how their roofs blew away, their pets were lost,
someone's cousin wandered off and drowned.

On Hollyberry, one oak leveled a car and a house.
Gas lines stretched for miles, entangling raw nerves.

Cutting through our anxieties condensing in the cold air
with the freezing snow, they came from New Mexico,
they came from Kentucky, Missouri, Wisconsin too,
volunteers from across the country, even from Canada,
they had driven in their trucks for days and nights
to hoist up our hopes, as they elevated themselves
in cranes to disarm the towering, weaponed trees,
to disentangle and heal the raw power lines.
Libraries and school gyms offered warmth and shelter,
while those who had gave Hefty bagfuls of sweaters,
wishing, "May the force be with you!"
and some connected their homes to their neighbors',
their electric umbilicals taped across the streets
into each other's portable generators for heat and light.
Yogurt places offered free phone charges and such,
and people took each other in, "For better or worse,
I got my in-laws living with me! Who knows how long?"
Parents moved back with grown children, babies
with grandparents, folks with those they got to know.
Our son's friend, newly divorced, stayed with us,
and a lone, disoriented seagull, Cid, ate from our cats' bowl
alongside Eric the Red cardinal, who lost Buttons, his mate.
Our son called us daily from DC, and we told him
he shouldn't feel he needed a hurricane to phone so much.
And I gave Mike a gift—"Her name is Sandy!" I said,
an amaryllis bulb, a promise for flowers in red and white,
red for the pulsing commotion of our lives
and white for every color of our needs and dependencies
fused to upwelling from debris with stubborn, astonishing beauty.

ABOUT GAYL TELLER

Nassau County Poet Laureate for 2009-2011 and the Walt Whitman Birthplace Association 2016 Poet of the Year, Gayl Teller received an MA from Columbia University and another MA from Queens College, CUNY. Her six poetry collections are *At the Intersection of Everything You Have Ever Loved, Shorehaven, Moving Day, One Small Kindness, Inside the Embrace,* and *Hidden in Plainview.* She is the editor of *Toward Forgiveness, An Anthology of Poems* (Writers Ink Press, 2011).

Internationally and widely published, her poems have appeared in *Poem, The South Coast Poetry Journal, Phoebe, The Nassau County Poet Laureate Society Review, Prosopisia: An International Journal of Poetry and Creative Writing, Front Range Review, RCC Muse, The Sow's Ear Poetry Journal, Paterson Literary Journal, Freshet, Poetrybay: Long Island Quarterly, Spring, Swansea Review, The Second Genesis, Newsday, The Long Islander:Walt's Corner, The Hartford Courant,* and in many other distinguished publications. Director and founder of the Poetry Reading Series, under the auspices of the New York State Council on the Arts, at the Mid-Island Y JCC, in Plainview, NY, for the past twenty-three years, she reviews the works of feature poets and judges the annual poetry contest for children, teens, and adults. She has been teaching in the English department of Hofstra University since 1985. As Nassau County Poet Laureate, she originated "Stray Feet," a roving poetry show visiting schools, senior and rehab centers, nursing homes, and libraries in Nassau County, and in 2010, her workshops/anthology project "A Poetry of Forgiveness" was awarded a NY State Council on the Arts Decentralization Grant for the Arts, which culminated in her editing *Toward Forgiveness,* an anthology of 99 LI poets, including five poets laureate. She has conducted numerous poetry workshops and seminars and been the feature reader at many universities, poetry centers, theaters and libraries. She serves as a mentor in the Nassau County Poet Laureate's Poetry Mentoring Program, and she has served as a judge in the Poetry Out Loud National Recitation Contest, which encourages the nation's youth to learn about great poetry through memorization and performance. She is the recipient of the Westmoreland Arts & Heritage Poetry Award, the Edgar Allan Poe Prize, the Peninsula Library Poetry Prize, a National Federation of State Poetry Societies Prize, a National League of American PEN Women Prize, and *The Connecticut Writer* Prize. In 2011, she received The North Sea Poetry Scene Recognition Award and in 2012, the Special Service Award from the Mid-Island Y JCC. Her poems are widely published and anthologized, and her reviews of poetry books have appeared frequently in *Small Press Review, Book/Mark* and other publications.

Her website is www.gaylteller.com.